GUIDE TO RESOURCES IN
ETHNIC STUDIES ON MINORITY POPULATIONS

GUIDE TO RESOURCES IN
ETHNIC STUDIES ON MINORITY POPULATIONS

Tyson Gibbs
and
Amy Frishkey

The Edwin Mellen Press
Lewiston•Queenston•Lampeter

Library of Congress Cataloging-in-Publication Data

Gibbs, Tyson.
    Guide to resources in ethnic studies on minority populations / Tyson Gibbs and Amy Frishkey.
    p. cm.
    ISBN 0-7734-7617-2
    1. Minorities--Study and teaching--United States--Directories. 2. United States--Ethnic
relations--Study and teaching--Directories. I. Frishkey, Amy. II. Title.

E184.A1 G46 2000

00-064560

A CIP catalog record for this book is available from the British Library.

The Edwin Mellen Press
Box 450
Lewiston, New York
USA 14092-0450

The Edwin Mellen Press
Box 67
Queenston, Ontario
CANADA L0S 1L0

The Edwin Mellen Press, Ltd.
Lampeter, Ceredigion, Wales
UNITED KINGDOM SA48 8LT

Printed in the United States of America

TABLE OF CONTENTS

Guide to Resources in Ethnic Studies

Introduction

The study of ethnic populations in the United States has been less systematic over most of the history of this country. The reason is a simple one. There was very little interest in ethnic minority populations as an area of research. There are numerous documents which describe the various ethnic groups in the United States. The federal, state and local governments kept some records on the various populations and their occupations beginning in the 1700's. Various individuals, "Travelers" would write about the different groups encountered while crossing the United States. Some of the various ethnic populations kept their own records of the issues confronting their group. For example one might find writings on Jews living in the major cities in the north or isolated populations in Southern towns. Germans living in the South or some Native American Groups, like the Cherokee, kept their own records. Amongst the Southern Plantation owners, detailed records were often kept on the activities taking place on the farm. Not only can one read about the transactions occurring related to the various slaves, but often the private thoughts about the Planter's Family, political issues of the day or other slave owners may be recorded in these Journals, making them an extremely valuable source of information. But these aren't systematic studies. These are isolated, individual documents.

This Guide is written to give the reader a direction whereby information can be found about the various ethnic groups listed The ethnic groups listed here are the larger minority populations. The material below was taken from the recent brief description of ethnic populations for the 2000 Census. It details how the data from the Census Bureau will be grouped; but also provided is information about how one might began the task of classifying ethnic and racial populations. The (Census Bureau Census 2000, " Data Products At a Glance") writes:

"The racial and ethnic makeup of the country has changed since 1977, giving rise to the question of whether those standards still reflected the diversity of the country's present population. In response to this criticism, the OMB initiated a review of the Directive. This review included (1) organizing a workshop to address the issues by the National Academy of Science, (2) convening four public hearings, and (3) appointing an Interagency Committee for the Review of Racial and Ethnic Standards, which later developed a research agenda and conducted several research studies. The result of the Committee's efforts was a report describing recommended changes to the Directive. The members of the Committee included representatives of more than 30 agencies that covered the many diverse federal requirements for data on race and ethnicity. In 1997, the OMB accepted almost all of the recommendations of the Interagency Committee, resulting in changes to the standards.

What Are The New Standards And When Do They Take Effect?

In October 1997, the Office of Management and Budge (OMB) announced the revised standards for federal data on race and ethnicity. The minimum categories for race are now: American Indian or Alaska Native: Asian: Black or African American: Native Hawaiian or Other Pacific Islander: and White. Instead of allowing a multiracial category as was originally suggested in public and congressional hearings, the OMB adopted the Interagency Committee's recommendation to allow respondents to select one or more races when they self-identify. With the OMB's approval, the Census 2000 questionnaires also include a sixth racial category: Some Other Race. There are also two minimum categories for ethnicity: Hispanic or Latino and Not Hispanic or Latino. Hispanics and Latinos may be of any race.

The new categories were used by the Census Bureau for the Census 2000 Dress Rehearsal in spring 1998, and will be used on the Census 2000 questionnaire. The new standards are effective immediately for new and revised data collections by federal agencies, and all federal agencies must implement the new standards by January 1, 2003.

How Does the Census 2000 Question on Race Differ from the 1990 Question?

The most profound change to the question on race for Census 2000 is than respondents are allowed to identify one or more races to indicate their racial identity. There are 15 check box response categories and 3 write-in areas on the Census 2000 questionnaire, compared with 16 check box response categories and 2 write-in areas in 1990. The three separate identifiers for the American Indian and Alaska Native populations (American Indian, Eskimo, or Aleut) used earlier have been combined into one category—American Indian or Alaska Native—with the instructions for respondents who check the box to print the name of their enrolled or principal tribe. The Asian and Pacific Islander category has been split into two categories Asian, and Native Hawaiian and Other Pacific Islander. There are six specified Asian and three detailed Pacific Islander categories shown on the Census 2000 questionnaires, as well as Other Asian and Other Pacific Islander which have write-in areas for respondents to provide other race responses. Finally, the category Some Other Race, which is intended to capture responses such as Mulatto, Creole, and Mestizo, also has a write-in area. All of the responses collected in Census 2000 can be collapsed into the minimum race categories identified in the 1997 revisions to the standards on race and ethnicity issued by the Office of Management and Budget, plus the category Some Other Race.

Other changes include terminology and formatting changes, such as spelling out "American" instead of "Amer." for the American Indian or Alaska Native category: and adding "Native" to the Hawaiian response category. In the layout of the Census 2000 questionnaire, the Asian response categories were alphabetized and grouped together, as were the Pacific Islander categories after the Native Hawaiian category. American Indians and Alaska Natives can report one or more tribes. In addition, the question on Hispanic origin is sequenced immediately before the question on race.

How Will the Data on Race from Census 2000 be Tabulated?

In 1997, the Office of Management and Budget (OMB) issued preliminary guidelines on how data for respondents who report two or more races are to be tabulated. These guidelines stipulated that data producers should provide the number of respondents who marked (or selected) only one category, separately for each of the five racial categories, as well as the detailed distribution of respondents who reported two or more races, so long as data quality standards and confidentiality requirements are met.

For Census 2000, 63 possible combinations of the six basic racial categories exist, including six categories for those who report exactly one race, and 57 categories for those who report two or more races. These categories will be the basic presentation for the PL 94-171 Redistricting File.

In some other presentations, the 57 combinations of two or more races will be collapsed into a category called "Two or More Races," resulting in seven mutually exclusive and exhaustive racial categories: American Indian and Alaska Native alone, Asian alone, Black or African American alone, Native Hawaiian and Other Pacific Islander alone, Some Other Race alone, White alone, and Two or More Races. This approach is a tally of all respondents and sums to 100 percent of the total population."

What is A Minority Population

From the early 1950s, through the mid-1960s, Americans considered the United States a "melting pot," a place where people from around the world mixed, and became American. The prevalent view during this roughly fifteen-year period was that anyone, regardless of country of origin, could prosper economically using the unwritten guiding principles of the work ethic. The work ethic principles stressed diligence to one's job honesty in business transactions and loyalty to the company that hired you. This idealized view of the American society as a melting pot was shattered by Glazer and Moynihan (1963), who studied immigrants from different countries who lived in New York City. They discovered that third-generation children (who looked like their parents, used the same language as their parents, and ate the same foods as their older relatives), voted differently, felt differently about issues of education and male/female relationships (Peoples & Bailey 1991:373). In effect, they were essentially as different from one another as their grandparents were from their ancestors. What Glazer and Moynihan discovered was that America was not a melting pot, and that the strength found in groups bonding together because of national origin, language, religious beliefs, customs, or group traditions were the ties that maintained ethnic boundaries (Peoples & Bailey 1991). Attempts to fully integrate and assimilate different cultural groupings by labeling them American, accomplished little toward breaking the protective effects that these groups found by maintaining their cultural roots. This study of the immigrant population living in New York City eventually resulted in the concept of ethnic minority.

The Ethnic Minority Group

An ethnic minority population is distinguished from the majority population by internal adoption, and practice, of customs, religion, dress, food habits, language, and values that promote group cohesiveness. The majority population will often distinguish ethnic minority group members by attributes that are easily identifiable—skin tone, dress, language, and perceived behavior. The adoption of easily identifiable attributes for ethnic minorities by the majority population promotes the idea of "we" and "they." Ethnic minority group members, to successfully compete for survival with the majority population, generally will take one of three options. The first is an attempt at imitating the value system, customs, language, and cultural behaviors of the majority population. Such attempts at survival can result in a measure of success by the ethnic minority members if the majority population accepts their actions. Adopting the customary behaviors of the majority population can also result in ostracism from fellow ethnic minority group members, because such actions can be viewed as traitorous. The second option for successful competition with the majority population is for the ethnic minority group member to promote their cultural heritage through ceremony, dress, food habits, language, or other distinguishable behaviors that set their group apart from the majority population. Such action from the ethnic minority group further supports the "we" and "they" concept, providing the majority population with information for purposes of acceptance, because the majority can clearly see difference, and the differences are something tolerable, or the majority can reject the ethnic minority group because the differences are more than the majority population is to accept. The last option is for the ethnic minority group to attempt to live in both cultures by adopting habits from their own minority group and habits from the majority population. Attempts to survive using the "foot in each camp" method generally place the ethnic group member as an outsider in both populations. African-American populations are distinguished by their participation, as ethnic minority group members, in all of the options described above. The internal struggle for survival by African-Americans using these options, in addition to their usually easy identification because of their skin tone, makes them the classic ethnic minority population. In American society, any group that bears the phenotype or outward skin tone of shades of light brown to very dark will bear the label of

African American, and, in general, such ascription will imply negative behavioral attributes.

The Cultural Minority

The concept of a cultural minority is to describe population groups that have limited access to power. Cultural minority group members are distinguishable by ascription of the majority population and by self-identification. The majority population maintains power and control through promoting the differences between cultural minority groups, their purported goals, and the agenda of the majority population as incompatible activities. The cultural minority group members may seek to achieve shared power though a promotion of their population needs when such needs can be identified as resulting from the lack of attention from the majority population. All African-Americans have been ascribed values and goals by the majority population that are stated as incompatible with the national concept of being an American. Such ascriptions are the stuff that promotes the ethnic minority group members as one single-minded body, incapable of assimilation into the value stream of the typical American. In effect, African-Americans are systematically kept from power through this technique of promoting value differences between them and the majority white population.

A Racial Minority

The concept of racial minorities promotes the visible skin distinctions between population groups living in the United States. Such distinctions are developed, formulated, and used by the majority population to maintain distances between groups. Recent Louis Harris polls taken over the last ten years, 1985 through 1995, continually point out that in America, both the majority white population and the minority African-American population do believe that the perceived differences between them keep the two groups apart. Racial minorities are distinguishable by their ascribes skin tones—yellow (Asian), black (African), brown (Hispanic), or red (Native American). Such attributes as "colors" are blurred in 1990s American society as a result of admixture of the different population groups over the last 400 plus years. Yet, many minority group members refer to themselves as black or brown to promote unity within the group. African-Americans and some Hispanic Americans have used the color label to identify themselves with their countries of origin or their perceived political unity.

Purpose

The purpose of this document is to provide information about resources currently available on Ethnic Minority populations. These resources include libraries and archival resources, popular media, colleges and universities, special programs, special centers, publishers, government programs, and journals.

Each resource has been developed in the following ways:

1.) Libraries and archival resources

In this category, we will: a.) list the resources, with some appearing in more than one category as they overlap (e.g., libraries within special centers); and b.) describe any special collections

2.) Popular media resources

We assume "popular media" to mean magazines, newspapers, Internet, radio, television, and film resources. In this category, we will: a.) list the resources; and b.) include a brief description of each.

3.) Colleges and universities

In this category, we are dealing with institutions that have historically and continue presently to cater their recruitment to the ethnic minorities of this pamphlet. In this category, we will: a.) list the colleges and universities; b.) list their status (public/private) and religious affiliation; c.) describe the quantity of their library holdings; d.) list their highest enrollments according to major; and ii describe the quantity of undergraduate and graduate students.

4.) Special Programs

In this category, we will list: a.) ethnic studies and specific minority studies programs; and b.) include a brief description of each.

5.) Special Centers

In this category, we will: a.) list the centers, with some appearing in more than one category as they overlap (for example, special centers within universities, as homes for special programs, etc.); and b) include a brief description of each.

6.) Publishers

In this category, we deal with publishers who concentrate on minority audiences and authors. We will: a.) list the publishers; and b.) include a brief description of each.

7.) *Government Programs*

In this category, we will focus on government agencies that deal with minority research and education. We will: a.) list the agencies; and b.) include a brief description of each agency's function. Each program is listed hierarchically (e.g., as part of an executive department), so that the reader will be familiar with each agency's chain of command.

8.) *Journals*

This category deals primarily with academic journals concerned with minority issues. We will: a.) list the journals; and b.) include a brief description of e iii

In using a resource's own words to its description, we have implemented *italics* in order for there to be no question concerning authorship.

Preface

Because of the growing demand for multicultural awareness to shaping bodies such as schools, government and media outlets, programs designed to deal with ethnic issues exist in nearly every entity that falls into these domains. The purpose of this book is to collect and describe these programs, arranging entries according to the sphere in which they fall and by the ethnic groups to which they pertain.

Information about ethnic resources is divided into five ethnic groups: African-American, Asian-American, Hawaiian/Pacific Islander, Hispanic/Latino American and American Indian. The book further categorizes programs by academic, governmental, publishing or media orientation. The data had its origins in a variety of sources, foremost among them the original sources and the Internet, which contain a tremendous amount of information about ethnic studies.

The authors deliberately examine governmental agencies to discern the main sources of the information. Because branch agencies frequently re-name themselves and shift personnel and location, the authors situated the agencies hierarchically within the federal government.

The book is structured so that the listings therein constitute a starting point for research into various facets of ethnicity. Accordingly, a large part of it is devoted to publishing contact information and Internet addresses for quick perusal of the contents of these programs. This guide does not contain a fairly comprehensive catalogue of resources. It fills a void by creating directories that are pertinent to ethnic studies in a variety of minority populations.

This book is timely and important. First, the dilemmas of racial/ethnic groups remain an important issue in the 21st century. A resource is needed that describes programs in schools, governments, and media outlets. Second, as the globe continues to shrink, networks of communication, immigration, trade, and transportation continues to link people into a global entity, the issues of diversity will become more international in scope, resulting in the need for directories targeted to diverse populations.

Erma Jean Lawson, Ph.D.
Harvard University Research Lecturer
School of Public Health
Boston, Massachusetts

I. African-Americans

Libraries and Archival Resources

African Bibliographic Center
Staff Resource Library
1346 Connecticut Ave., NW, Room 901
Washington, DC 20036

African Studies Library
Boston University
Gretchen Walsh: (617) 353-3726
E-mail: gwalsh@acs.bu.edu

Houses 144,000 volumes and African government documents, 1000 current and past periodical titles, 30 current newspaper subscriptions and over 100 newspaper titles on microfilm, 3100 pamphlets, and a map collection. Staffs 2 full-time Africana librarians.

The Africana Collection
The Michigan State University Library
Phone: (517) 355-2366
Acting Africana Librarian: Professor Joseph Lauer
Phone: (517) 432-2218
E-mail: lauer@pilot.msu.edu

Houses over 200,000 books, pamphlets, maps, and microformat units, and over 3510 serial titles.

Africana Reading Room
The University of Illinois Library

328 Main Library
1408 W. Gregory Dr.
Urbana, IL 61801
Phone: (217) 333-6519
Hours: 8:30am - 5pm, M-F

Houses approximately 160,000 volumes, 2500 journals, 46,000 maps, and 10,000 microforms. *Especially strong in a broad range of European journals that include articles on Africa from the 19th century to the present.* The Room contains indexes, bibliographies, handbooks, directories, and other references materials pertaining to Africa.

The Afro-American Cultural and Historical Society
1839 E. 81st St.
Cleveland, OH 44103

The Afro American Historical Society Museum
1841 Kennedy Blvd.
Jersey City, NJ 07305
Phone: (201) 547-5262
Fax: (201) 547-5392

Organized by Captain Thomas Taylor, President of the Jersey City Branch of the NAACP, for *the research, collection, preservation, and exhibition of Afro-American history and culture.*

Amistad Research Center
Tilton Hall - Tulane University
6823 St. Charles Ave.
New Orleans, LA 70118
Reference: (504) 862-3222

Voice: (504) 865-5535
Internet: amistad@tulane.edu

Organized in 1966, the center emerged as the first institution created to document the civil rights movement. It is acknowledged today as the nation's largest independent African-American archives. Includes oral history and video collections, a specialized library, travelling exhibits, publications, and art.

The Annenberg School of Communications Library
University of Pennsylvania
4025 Chestnut St.
Philadelphia, PA 19104-3054
Phone: (215) 898-7027

Contains an ethnographic film collection with material on Africa.

Association of the Study of Afro-American Life and History Library
1401 14th St., NW
Washington, DC 20005

Black Studies Division
Martin Luther King Memorial Library
District of Columbia Public Library
901 G St., NW
Washington, DC 20001

Black Studies Library
Ohio State University
1858 Nei Ave.
Columbus, OH 43210

Center for Research Libraries
Ohio University Libraries
Alden Library, 1st floor
Athens, OH 45701
Contact: Theodore (Ted) S. Foster, African Studies Bibliographer
Phone: (740) 593-2659
E-mail: fosterth@ohiou.edu

Designated as a Title IV National Resource Center for Africana, the Center provides links to the Cooperative Africana Microform Project (CAMP), which offers one of the largest collections of African newspapers on microform (Amy Bell, 1996).

Chicago Public Library Cultural Center
Vivian G. Harsh Collection of Afro-American History and Literature
9525 S. Haister St.
Chicago, IL 60628

Douglass-Truth Branch Library
Seattle Public Library
23rd Ave. & E. Yesier Way
Seattle, WA 98122

Du Sable Museum of African-American History - Library
740 E. 56th P.
Chicago, IL 60637

Hollis Burke Frissell Library - Archives
Tuskegee Institute
Tuskegee Institute, AL 36088

The John Henrik Clarke Africana Library
Cornell University
310 Triphammer Rd.
Ithaca, NY 14853
Service desk Phone: (607) 255-3822
Librarian: Thomas Weissinger, (607) 255-5229
Fax: (607) 255-0784
E-mail: afrlib-mailbox@cornell.edu

*Located in the Africana Studies and Research Center, where it supports research
and teaching activities. Collection focuses on history and cultures of peoples of
African ancestry in the Americas, Africa, and the Caribbean* (Amy Bell, 1996).

Langston Hughes Library and Cultural Center
Queens Borough Public Library
102-09 Northern Blvd.
Corona, NY 11368

Langston Hughes Memorial Library - Special Collection
Lincoln University
Lincoln University, PA 19352

Library of Congress - African Section
African & Middle Eastern Division
Jefferson Bldg., Room 220
Washington, DC 20540-4820
Phone: (202) 707-5528
Fax: (202) 252-3180
E-mail: amed@loc.gov

Contains extensive materials on sub-Saharan Africa. *One of the best collections in the world, particularly strong in economics, history, linguistics, and literature* (Amy Bell, 1996).

The Melville J. Herskovits Library of African Studies
Northwestern University - Evanston Campus
1935 Sheridan Rd.
Evanston, IL 60208-3084
Reference desk Phone: (847) 491-7684 (from 8:30am-5pm, M-F)
Office Phone: (847) 491-7684
Fax: (847) 491-8306
E-mail: africana@nwu.ed
Curator: David L. Eastbrook, dleaster@nwu.edu

Contains a large collection of Africana in all media forms, with the largest separate African Studies library in the world. Houses 245,000 volumes, 2800 current serials, 300 current newspapers, 10,500 books in 300 different African languages, archival and manuscript collections, maps, posters, videos, and electronic resources.

Melvine E. Tolson Black Heritage Center
Langston University
Page Hall Annex, 2nd floor
Langston, OK 73050

Museum of Afro American History
Abiel Smith School
46 Joy St.
Boston, MA 02114
Phone: (617) 742-1854
Fax: (617) 742-3589

Hours: T-F, 10am-4pm
Admission: Free

Educational institution founded for the study of New England Afro American communities and to promote awareness of the area. Built around the first public school for blacks in the country.

National Museum of African Art Branch
Smithsonian Institution Libraries
950 Independence Ave. SW, MRC 708
Washington, DC 20560
Phone: (202) 357-4600, ext.286
Fax: (202) 357-4879

Focuses on visual arts, with supporting collections of history, archeology, religion, oral traditions, music, and literature. A monthly list of new publications is distributed without charge (Smithsonian Institution Libraries).

The Robert S. Rankin Civil Rights Memorial Library
624 9th St. NW
Washington, DC 20425
Phone: (202) 376-8128
Hours: 10am-4pm, M-F

Library collection houses *50,000 reference works, including 150 civil rights and minority issues journals, periodicals, legal journals, newspapers, 4000 reels of microfilm and files of microfiche, and a comprehensive collection of reports, transcripts, and civil rights texts.* Also houses 2 on-line database systems: Ohio College Library Center (OCLC) and Lexis/Nexis.

Stanford University - Africana Libraries

Hoover Library

Karen Fung, Deputy Curator

Tower - Room 212

Phone: (415) 725-3505

E-mail: fung@hoover.stanford.edu

Stanford University Libraries

John Rawlings, Africa bibliographer

Green Library Reference Department

Phone: (415) 723-3101

E-mail: cn.jwr@forsythe.stanford.edu

Stanford offers an excellent collection of British documents on Africa. In addition, Stanford collects official African documents, a majority of which emanate from English-speaking Central and Southern Africa. Karen Fung has developed a wonderful web site, Africa South of Sahara: Selected Internet Resources, including an international list of Libraries and Archives specializing in Africana material, with direct telnet links. (Amy Bell, 1996)

The University of California at Berkeley Africana and African-American Collection

Phyllis Bischoff, Bibliographer

Much of the collection is located in the Doe Library, with rich holdings in African serials and documents, as well as African studies material published in the Soviet Union since WW II. Geographic strengths include Botswana, Egypt, Kenya, Nigeria (especially the Yoruba region), South Africa, and Zambia. Languages collected include Arabic, Swahili, Yoruba, and major European languages. (Amy Bell, 1996)

The University of California at Los Angeles - African Library Resources
Ruby Bell-Gam, bibliographer
Internet: http://www.isop.ucla.edu/jscasc/resource/library.htm

The University Research Library has a substantial African Studies collection, supporting its James S. Coleman African Studies Center. It also holds the Roland Stevenson manuscripts of African languages, making it one of the best resources for African linguistics research. (Amy Bell, 1996)

Yale University - African Collection
Sterling Memorial Library, Room 317
120 High St.
New Haven, CT
Phone: (203) 432-1883
Hours: 8:30am-5pm, M-F
Internet: http://www.library.yale.edu/africa.html

The African Collection at Sterling Memorial Library is, like many of Yale's collections, large and very rich. Particular strengths include Southern Africa, and French-speaking west and central Africa. (Amy Bell, 1996)

Popular Media

African Arts Magazine
Donald J. Cosentino & Doran H. Ross, editors
Phone: (310) 825-1218
Fax: (310) 206-2250
E-mail: afriarts@ucla.edu

Exclusively devoted to the arts of Africa and its Diaspora.

African Films at the University of Florida

Internet: http://web.africa.ufl.edu/films/filmlist.html

Films are housed at different locations on campus

Website African Media Program Online Database

Internet: http://www.isp.msu.edu/AfricanStudies/AFMedia/AMP_page1.htm

Provides a comprehensive on-line reference guide to films, videos, and other audiovisual materials on Africa.

Website California Newsreel's Library of African Cinema

Internet: http://www.newsreel.org

Provides reviews and articles pertaining to film titles.

Colleges/Universities

Alabama Agricultural and Mechanical University

PO Box 411

Normal, AL 35762

Phone: (205) 851-5673

Fax: (205) 851-5030

Internet: http://www.aamu.edu

public, land-grant, non-sectarian university

- library collection houses 339,272 volumes, 1606 periodical subscriptions, and 488,759 microform items
- highest enrollments: business administration, education, and computer science

- approximately 3958 undergraduates and 1330 graduate students (full-time enrollment)

Alabama State University

PO Box 271

Montgomery, AL 36101-0271

Phone: (334) 229-4100

Admissions Contact: Billy Brooks, M.Ed.

- public, non-sectarian university
- library collection houses 226,907 volumes, 1,111 periodical subscriptions, and 365,336 microform items
- highest enrollments: accounting, elementary education, and criminal justice
- approximately 4159 undergraduates and 438 graduate students

Albany State University

504 College Dr.

Albany, GA 31705

Phone: (912) 430-4604

Fax: (912) 430-3836

Admissions Contact: Kathleen Caldwell, MS, (912) 430-4646

- public, non-sectarian liberal arts college
- Library collection houses 180,000 volumes, 1066 periodical subscriptions, and 15,787 microform items.
- highest enrollments: criminal justice, nursing, and accounting
- approximately 2208 undergraduates and 303 graduate students

Alcorn State University

PO Box 359

Lorman, MS 39096

Phone: (601) 877-6111

Fax: (601) 877-2975

Admissions Contact: Emanuel Barnes, MS, (601) 877-6147, or 1-800-222-6790

- public, land-grant, non-sectarian university
- Library collection houses 168,058 volumes, 964 periodicals subscriptions, 368,927 microfilm items, and 7 CD-ROM titles.
- highest enrollments: business, agricultural economics, and biology
- approximately 2345 undergraduates and 187 graduate students

Allen University

Office of Enrollment Management

1530 Harden St.

Columbia, SC 29204

Phone: (803) 376-5701

Fax: (803) 376-5709

E-mail: auniv@mindspring.com

- private university affiliated with the African Methodist Episcopal Church
- approximately 250 enrolled full-time

Arkansas Baptist College

1600 Bishop St.

Little Rock, AR 72202

Phone: (501) 372-6883

Fax: (501) 372-0321

- private liberal arts college affiliated with American Baptist Churches in the USA
- approximately 411 undergraduates

Barber-Scotia College

145 Cabarrus Ave.

Concord, NC 28025

Phone: (704) 789-2900

Fax: (704) 789-2958

Admissions Contact: Abbie Butler

- private liberal arts college affiliated with the Presbyterian Church USA
- library collection houses 26,356 volumes, 193 periodical subscriptions, and 1100 microform items
- highest enrollments: sociology, business administration, and biology
- approximately 704 undergraduates

Benedict College

600 Harden St.

Columbia, SC 29204

Phone: (803) 254-7253

Fax: (803) 253-5060

Admissions Contact: Wanda Scott, MA, (803) 253-5143, or 1-800-868-6598

- private liberal arts college affiliated with the Baptist Church; 2 semesters of religion required, chapel attendance mandatory
- library collection houses 134,167 volumes, 573 periodical subscriptions, and 37,065 microform items
- highest enrollments: business administration, criminal justice, and social work
- approximately 1850 enrolled full-time

Bennett College

900 E. Washington St.

Greensboro, NC 27401

Phone: (910) 370-8626

Fax: (910) 272-7143

Admissions Contact: Yolanda Johnson

Phone: (910) 370-8624

- private woman's college, affiliated with United Methodist Church; 3 semester hours
- of religion/theology required
- library collection houses 95,293 volumes, 325 periodical subscriptions, and 1800 microform items
- highest enrollments: business administration, education, and interdisciplinary studies
- approximately 650 female undergraduates

Bethune-Cookman College

640 Dr. Mary McLeod Bethune Blvd.

Daytona Beach, FL 32114-3099

Phone: (904) 252-8667

Fax: (904) 257-7027

Admissions Contact: Catherine Cook, PhD, (904) 238-3803, or 1-800-448-0228

- affiliated with the United Methodist Church; 2 semesters of religion required
- library collection houses 149,108 volumes, 770 periodical subscriptions, 38,691 microform items, and 25 CD-ROM titles
- highest enrollments: business administration, criminal justice, and elementary education
- approximately 2233 undergraduates

Bishop State Community College

351 N. Broad St.

Mobile, AL 36603

Phone: (334) 690-6416

Fax: (334) 438-9523

Bluefield State College

219 Rock St.

Bluefield, WV 24701

Phone: (304) 327-4030

Fax: (304) 325-7747

Admissions Contact: John C. Cardwell, MA, (304) 327-4065

- public, African-American teacher's college, non-sectarian
- library collection houses 108,490 volumes, 524 periodical subscriptions, and 242,251 microform items
- highest enrollments: business administration, education, and criminal justice
- approximately 1463 undergraduates

Bowie State University

14000 Jericho Park Rd.

Bowie, MD 20715

Phone: (301) 464-6500

Fax: (301) 464-7814

Admissions Contact: Dharmi Chaudhari, (301) 464-6570

- public, non-sectarian university of liberal arts and technology studies
- library collection houses 255,282 volumes, 1287 periodical subscriptions, and 598,007 microform items
- highest enrollments: business administration, communications media, and elementary education
- approximately 2185 undergraduates and 3238 graduate students

Central State University

1400 Brushrow Rd.

Wilberforce, OH 45384

Phone: (513) 376-6332

Fax: (513) 376-6530

Admissions Contact: Robert E. Johnson, Med

Phone: (513) 376-6348

- comprehensive, non-sectarian, public university
- library collection houses 155,643 volumes, 890 periodical subscriptions, and 555,443 microform items
- highest enrollments: business administration and education
- approximately 2304 undergraduates and 18 graduate students

Cheyney University of Pennsylvania

Cheyney, PA 19319

Phone: (610) 399-2220

Fax: (610) 399-2415

Admissions Contact: Sharon Cannon, MA, 1-800-CHEYNEY

- public, non-sectarian university
- library collection houses 237,780 volumes, 655 periodical subscriptions, 517,955 microform items
- highest enrollments: business administration, education, and social relations
- approximately 911 undergraduates and 324 graduate students

Chicago State University

Chicago, IL 60628

Phone: (312) 995-2000

Admissions Contact: Romi Lowe, (312) 995-2513

- public, non-sectarian university

- library collection houses over 270,000 volumes, 1377 periodical subscriptions, and 513,941 microform items
- highest enrollments: accounting, early childhood elementary education, and nursing
- approximately 4611 undergraduates and 2692 graduate students

City University of New York, Medgar Evans College
Brooklyn, NY 11225
Phone: (718) 270-4900
Admissions Contact: Roberta Danneselser, PhD
Phone: (718) 270-6024

- public, non-sectarian university
- library collection houses 77,568 volumes
- approximately 2882 undergraduates

City University of New York, NYC Technical College
Brooklyn, NY 11201-2983
Phone: (718) 260-5000
Admissions Contact: Arlene Matsumoto Floyd, MBA, (718) 260-5500

- public, non-sectarian university
- library collection houses 169,771 volumes and 930 periodical subscriptions
- approximately 7325 undergraduates

City University of New York, York College
Jamaica, NY 11451
Phone: (718) 262-2000
Admissions Contact: Sally Nelson, MA, (718) 212-2165

- public, non-sectarian university

- Library collection houses over 153,000 volumes, 11,000 periodical subscriptions, and 110,000 microform items.
- highest enrollments: business administration, accounting, and information systems management
- approximately. 3891 undergraduates

Claflin College

700 College Ave., NE
Orangeburg, SC 29115
Phone: (803) 535-5412
Fax: (803) 535-5402
Admissions Contact: George Lee

- affiliated with the United Methodist Church, religious observance recommended
- approximately 904 undergraduates

Clark Atlanta University

James P. Brawley Dr., SW at Fair St.
Atlanta, GA 30314
Phone: (404) 880-8500
Fax: (404) 880-8995
Admissions Contact: Clifton B. Rawles, MA
Phone: (404) 880-8017

- private university affiliated with the United Methodist Church
- Library collection houses over 750,000 volumes.
- approximately 3764 undergraduates and 1279 graduate students

Clinton Junior College

1029 Crawford Rd.

Rock Hill, SC 29730

Phone: (803) 327-7402

Fax: (803) 327-3261

Coahoma Community College

3240 Friars Point Rd.

Clarksdale, MS 38614

Phone and Fax: (601) 627-2571

- public (district) junior college
- approximately 915 enrolled full-time

Concordia College

1804 Green St.

Selma, AL 36701

Phone: (334) 874-5708

Fax: (334) 874-5755

- private college affiliated with the Lutheran Church
- approximately 348 enrolled

Coppin State College

2500 West North Ave.

Baltimore, MD 21216

Phone: (410) 383-5910

Fax: (410) 333-5369

Admissions Contact: Allen D. Mosley MS

Phone: (410) 383-5990

- public, non-sectarian college

- library collection houses 134,983 volumes, 665 periodical subscriptions, and 231,573 microform items
- highest enrollments: management science, psychology, and nursing
- approximately 2156 undergraduates and 424 graduate students

Delaware State University
1200 N. Dupont Hwy.
Dover, DE 19901-2275
Phone: (302) 739-4901
Fax: (302) 739-6292
Admissions Contact: Jethro C. Williams

- public, non-sectarian university
- library collection houses 179,082 volumes, 2850 periodical subscriptions, 81,482 microform items, 30 CD-ROM titles, and 5641 audiovisual items
- highest enrollments: business administration, marketing, and accounting
- approximately 2562 undergraduates and 240 graduate students

Denmark Technical College
PO Box 927
Denmark, SC 29042
Phone: (803) 793-3301
Fax: (803) 793-5942
Contact: Dr. Joann R.G. Boyd-Scotland

Dillard University
2601 Gentilly Blvd.
New Orleans, LA 70122
Phone: (504) 283-8822
Fax: (504) 288-8663
Internet: http://www.dillard.edu

Admissions Contact: Vernese B. O'Neal, MS

Phone: 1-800-216-6637

- private, liberal arts university; interdenominational Christian affiliation
- library collection houses over 144,000 volumes and 682 periodical subscriptions
- highest enrollments: business administration/accounting, pre-engineering, and mass communications
- approximately 1544 undergraduates

Drew University of Medicine and Science

1621 E. 120th St.

Los Angeles, CA 90059

Phone: (213) 563-4800

- private, non-sectarian university
- approximately 625 enrolled

J.F. Drake State Technical College

3421 Meridian St. N.

Huntsville, AL 35811

Phone: (205) 539-8161

Fax: (205) 539-6439

- public, non-sectarian college
- approximately 576 enrolled

Edward Waters College

1658 Kings Rd.

Jacksonville, FL 32209

Phone: (904) 366-2500

Fax: (904) 366-2544

- liberal arts college affiliated with the African Methodist Episcopal Church
- approximately 587 undergraduates

Elizabeth City State University

PO Box 790

Elizabeth City, NC 27909

Phone: (919) 335-3230

Fax: (919) 335-3731

Admissions Contact: Erthel Hines, M. Soc.Work, (919) 335-3305

- comprehensive, non-sectarian, public university
- Library collection houses 136,973 volumes, 1628 periodical subscriptions, and 434,574 microform items.
- highest enrollments: business administration, criminal justice, and elementary education
- approximately 1936 undergraduates

Fayetteville State University

1200 Murchinson Rd.

Fayetteville, NC 28301

Phone: (910) 486-1411

Fax: (910) 486-4732

Admissions Contact: James Scurry, MEd

Phone: (910) 486-1371

- public, non-sectarian university
- library collection houses 179,643 volumes, 1874 periodical subscriptions, and 469,944 microform items.
- highest enrollments: business administration, sociology, and education

- approximately 2632 undergraduates and 783 graduate students

Fisk University

1000 17th Ave. N.

Nashville, TN 37208

Phone: (615) 329-8555

Fax: (615) 329-8576

Admissions Contact: Harrison I. DeShields MA

Phone: (615) 329-8666

- non-denominational Christian liberal arts university
- library collection houses 186,174 volumes, 595 periodical subscriptions, and 4270 microform items
- highest enrollments: biology, psychology, and English

Florida A&M University

400 Lee Hall

Tallahassee, FL 32307

Phone: (904) 599-3225

Fax: (904) 561-2152

Admissions Contact: Barbara Cox

Phone: (904) 599-3796

- public, non-sectarian university
- library collection houses 485,985 volumes, 3300 periodical subscriptions, and 82,000 microform items
- highest enrollments: business administration and health professions
- approximately 8074 undergraduates and 543 graduate students

Florida Memorial College

15800 NW 42nd Ave.

Miami, FL 33054

Phone: (305) 626-3604

Fax: (305) 626-3769

Admissions Contact: Peggy Kelly

Phone: (305) 626-3750

- affiliated with the Baptist Church; 8 semester hours of religion required.
- highest enrollments: elementary education, business administration, and criminal justice
- approximately 1205 undergraduates

Fort Valley State College

1005 State College Dr.

Fort Valley, GA 31030

Phone: (912) 825-6315

Fax: (912) 825-6266

Admissions Contact: Myldred P. Hill, EdD

Phone: (912) 825-6307

- public, non-sectarian college
- library collection houses 190,062 volumes and 1213 periodical subscriptions

Fredd State Technical College

202 Skyline Blvd.

Tuscaloosa, AL 35401

Phone: (205) 758-3361

Fax: (205) 391-2311

Grambling State University

PO Box 607

Grambling, LA 71245

Phone: (318) 274-2211

Fax: (318) 274-2398

Admissions Contact: Nora D. Bingamen, MEd

Phone: (318) 274-2435

- public, non-sectarian university
- library collection houses over 227,000 volumes
- highest enrollments: business administration, criminal justice, and nursing
- approximately 7833 undergraduates and 598 graduate students

Hampton University

Hampton, VA 23368

Phone: (804) 727-5000

Fax: (804) 727-5746

Admissions Contact: Dr. Ollie M. Bowman

Phone: 1-800-624-3328 or (804) 727-5328

- private, non-sectarian university
- library collection houses over 235,000 volumes, 1200 periodical subscriptions, and 35,000 microform items
- highest enrollments: accounting, biology, and psychology
- approximately 4556 undergraduates and 396 graduate students

Harris-Stowe State College

3026 Laclede Ave.

St. Louis, MO 63103

Phone: (314) 340-3385

Fax: (314) 340-3399

Admissions Contact: Valerie A. Beeson MA

- public, non-sectarian college for educational studies

- library collection houses over 60,000 volumes
- highest enrollments: elementary school education
- approximately 850 undergraduates

Howard University

2400 6th St., NW

Washington, DC 20059

Phone: (202) 806-2500

Fax: (202) 806-5934

Admissions Contact: Rochetta Johnson

Phone: (202) 806-2752

- private, non-sectarian university
- library collection houses 1,900,000 volumes, 19,400 periodical subscriptions, and 2,266,115 microform items
- highest enrollments: electrical engineering, business administration, and communications
- approximately 6274 undergraduates and 5369 graduate students

Huston-Tillotson College

900 Chicon St.

Austin, TX 78702

Phone: (512) 505-3003

Fax: (512) 505-3190

Admissions Contact: Donnie J. Scott

Phone: (512) 505-3027 ext. 3028 or 3029

- interdenominational Christian college; attendance mandatory for chapel once a week
- library collection houses 80,406 volumes, 320 periodical subscriptions, and 73,011 microform items

- highest enrollments: business administration and sociology
- approximately 506 undergraduates

Interdenominational Theological Center
671 Beckwith St.
Atlanta, GA 30314
Phone: (404) 527-7702
Fax: (404) 527-0901

Jackson State University
PO Box 17390
1400 J.R. Lynch St.
Jacksonville, MS 39217
Phone: (601) 968-2323
Fax: (601) 968-2948
Admissions Contact: Stephanie Chatman
Phone: (601) 968-2100

- public, non-sectarian university
- library collection houses over 371,200 volumes and 2715 periodical subscriptions
- highest enrollments: business administration, accounting, and elementary education
- approximately 4694 undergraduates and 974 graduate students

Jarvis Christian College
US Hwy. 80
Hawkins, TX 75765
Phone: (903) 769-5700
Fax: (903) 769-4842

Johnson C. Smith University

100 Beatties Ford Rd.

Charlotte, NC 28216

Phone: (704) 378-1008

Fax: (704) 372-5746

Kentucky State University

Room 201, Hume Hall

East Main Street

Frankfort, KY 40601

Phone: (502) 227-6260

Fax: (502) 227-6490

Knoxville College

901 College St.

Knoxville, TN 37921

Phone: (615) 524-6514

Fax: (615) 524-6603

Lane College

545 Lane Ave.

Jackson, TN 38301

Phone: (901) 426-7595

Fax: (901) 427-3987

Langston University

PO Box 907

Langston, OK 73050

Phone: (405) 466-3388

Fax: (405) 466-3461

Lawson State Community College

3060 Wilson Rd., SW

Birmingham, AL 35221-1798

Phone: (205) 925-2515

Fax: (205) 929-6316

- public, non-sectarian university
- approximately 1701 undergraduates

LeMoyne-Owen College

807 Walker Ave.

Memphis, TN 38126

Phone: (901) 942-7301

Fax: (901) 942-3572

Lewis College of Business

17370 Myers Rd.

Detroit, MI 48235

Phone: (313) 862-6240

Fax: (313) 862-1027

Lincoln University

PO Box 29

Jefferson City, MS 63013

Phone: (314) 681-5042

Fax: (314) 681-6074

Lincoln University of Pennsylvania

PO Box 179

Lincoln, PA 19352

Admissions Contact: Ms. Janice Walker

Phone: (610) 932-8300

Fax: (610) 932-8316

Livingstone College

701 W. Monroe St.

Salisbury, NC 28144

Phone: (704) 638-5505

Fax: (704) 638-5522

Martin University

Indianapolis, IN 46218

Phone: (317) 543-3238

Admissions Contact: Bobbye Jean Craig

- private, non-sectarian liberal arts university
- approximately 324 undergraduates and 27 graduate students

Marygrove College

Detroit, MI 48221-2599

Phone: (313) 862-8000

Admissions Contact: Carla R. Stepp, MA

Phone: (313) 862-5200

- private college affiliated with the Roman Catholic Church; one semester of religion, theology, or philosophy required
- library collection houses over 195,573 volumes, 800 periodical subscriptions, 23,026 microform items, and 550 audiovisual items
- highest enrollments: business, computer science, and psychology
- approximately 551 undergraduates and 128 graduate students

Mary Holmes College

Hwy. 50 W., PO Drawer 1257

West Point, MS 39773

Phone: (601) 494-6820

Fax: (601) 494-1881

- private two-year college affiliated with the United Presbyterian Church
- approximately 403 enrolled

Meharry Medical College

1005 Dr. D.B. Todd, Jr. Blvd.

Nashville, TN 37208

Phone: (615) 327-6904

Fax: (615) 327-6540

Miles College

PO Box 3800

Birmingham, AL 35208

Phone: (205) 923-2771

Fax: (205) 923-9292

Mississippi Valley State University

14000 Hwy. 82 West

Ittabena, MS 38941

Phone: (601) 254-3425

Fax: (601) 254-6709

Morehouse College

830 Westview Dr., SW

Atlanta, GA 30314

Phone: (404) 215-2645

Fax: (404) 659-6536

Morehouse School of Medicine
720 Westview Dr., SW
Atlanta, GA 30310
Phone: (404) 752-1740
Fax: (404) 752-1180

Morgan State University
Cold Spring Lane and Hillen Road
Baltimore, MD 21239
Phone: (410) 319-3200
Fax: (410) 319-3107

Morris College
North Main St.
Sumter, SC 29150
Phone: (803) 775-9371
Fax: (803) 773-3687

Morris Brown College
643 M.L.K., Jr. Dr.
Atlanta, GA 30314
Phone: (404) 220-0100
Fax: (404) 659-4315

Norfolk State University
2401 Corprew Ave.
Norfolk, VA 23504
Phone: (804) 683-8670
Fax: (804) 683-2342

North Carolina Agriculture and Technical State University

1601 E. Market St.

Greensboro, NC 27411

Phone: (910) 334-7940

Fax: (910) 334-7082

Admissions Contact: John F. Smith MS

Phone: (910) 334-7946

- public, non-sectarian university
- highest enrollments: accounting, electrical engineering, and industrial technology
- approximately 6244 undergraduates and 996 graduate students

North Carolina Central University

1801 Fayetteville St.

Durham, NC 27707

Phone: (919) 560-6304

Fax: (919) 560-5014

Oakwood College

Oakwood Rd., NW

Huntsville, AL 35811

Phone: (205) 726-7334

Fax: (205) 726-7123

Paine College

1235 15th St.

Augusta, GA 30901

Phone: (706) 821-8230

Fax: (706) 821-8333

Paul Quinn College

3837 Simpson Stuart Rd.

Dallas, TX

Phone: (214) 376-1000

Fax: (214) 302-3559

Philander Smith College

812 W. 13th St.

Little Rock, AR 72202

Phone: (501) 370-5275

Fax: (501) 370-5278

Prairie View A&M University

PO Box 188

Prairie View, TX 77446-0188

Phone: (409) 857-2111

Fax: (409) 857-3928

Rust College

150 E. Rust Ave.

Holly Springs, MS 38635

Phone: (601) 252-2491

Fax: (601) 252-6107

Saint Augustine's College

1315 Oakwood Ave.

Raleigh, NC 27601

Phone: (919) 516-4200

Fax: (919) 828-0817

Saint Paul's College

Lawrenceville, VA 23868

Phone: (804) 848-3111

Admissions Contact: Mary Ransom

Phone: (804) 848-3984

- private college affiliated with the Protestant Episcopal Church; three semesters of religion or theology required
- library collection houses over 55,000 volumes, 225 periodical subscriptions, and 30,093
- microform items
- highest enrollments: sociology, business administration, and political science
- approximately 678 undergraduates

Saint Phillip's College
M.L.K., Jr. Dr.

San Antonio, TX 78203

Phone: (210) 531-3591

Fax: (210) 531-3590

Savannah State College
PO Box 20449

Savannah, GA 31404

Phone: (912) 356-2240

Fax: (912) 356-2998

Selma University
1501 Lapsley St.

Selma, AL 36701

Phone: (334) 872-2533

Fax: (334) 872-7746

Shaw University
118 E. South St.
Raleigh, NC 27611
Phone: (919) 546-8300
Fax: (919) 546-8301

Shorter College
604 Locust St.
North Little Rock, AR 72114
Phone: (501) 374-6305
Fax: (501) 374-9333

Sojourner-Douglass College
Baltimore, MD 21205
Phone: (410) 276-0306

- private, non-sectarian liberal arts college
- approximately 262 undergraduates

Southern University
PO Box 12596
Baton Rouge, LA 70813
Phone: (504) 771-4680
Fax: (504) 771-5522
Admissions Contact: Dr. Rose Glee

Southern University at New Orleans
6400 Press Dr.
New Orleans, LA 70128
Phone: (504) 286-5313
Fax: (504) 286-5131

Admissions Contact: Melvin L. Hodges

- public, non-sectarian university
- approximately 3300 undergraduates and 200 graduate students

Southern University at Shreveport/Bossier City

3050 M.L. King, Jr. Dr.

Shreveport, LA 71107

Phone: (318) 674-3312

Fax: (318) 674-3374

Admissions Contact: Dr. Anthony Molina

Southern University A&M College

PO Box 9374

Baton Rouge, LA 70813

Phone: (504) 771-5022

Fax: (504) 771-2018

- comprehensive, public, 4-year college
- The Camille Shade African-American Collection houses over 1 million volumes.
- approximately 9000 enrolled

South Carolina State University

300 College St., NE

Orangeburg, SC 29117

Phone: (803) 536-7013

Fax: (803) 533-3622

Southwestern Christian College

PO Box 10

Terrell, TX 75160

Phone: (972) 524-3341

Fax: (972) 563-7133

Admissions Contact: Gerald Lee

- liberal arts college with a 4-year religious education component
- affiliated with the Church of Christ

Spelman College

350 Spelman Ln., SW

Atlanta, GA 30314

Phone: (404) 223-1400

Fax: (404) 223-7523

E-mail: admiss@spelman.edu

private, independent liberal arts college for women

Stillman College

3706 Stillman Blvd.

PO Box 1430

Tuscaloosa, AL 35403

Phone: (205) 349-4240

Fax: (205) 758-0821

Internet: http://www.stillman.edu

- private, 4-year liberal arts college affiliated with the Presbyterian Church USA
- approximately 1014 enrolled

Talladega College

627 W. Battle St.

Talladega, AL 35160

Phone: (205) 761-6212

Fax: (205) 362-2268

- private, 4-year college
- approximately 615 undergraduates

Tennessee State University

Office of Public Relations

3500 John A. Merritt Blvd., Campus Box 9591

Nashville, TN 37209

Phone: (615) 963-7401

Fax: (615) 963-7407

Comprehensive, urban, land-grant university.

Texas College

PO Box 4500

Tyler, TX 75202

Phone: (903) 593-8311

Fax: (903) 593-0588

Texas Southern University

3100 Cleburne Ave.

Houston, TX 77004

Phone: (713) 313-7034

Fax: (713) 639-1092

- comprehensive urban university
- library collection houses over 452,850 books and 349,969 microform items
- approximately 10,000 students

Tougaloo College

500 E. County Line Rd.

Tougaloo, MS 39174

Phone: (601) 977-7730

Fax: (601) 977-7739

E-mail: information@mail.tougaloo.edu

Private, liberal arts college with interdenominational Christian affiliation.

Trenholm State Technical College

1225 Air Base Blvd.

Montgomery, AL 36108

Phone: (334) 832-9000

Fax: (334) 832-9777

Tuskegee University

102 Old Administration Bldg.

Tuskegee, AL 36088

Internet: www.tusk.edu

Phone: (334) 727-8501

Fax: (334) 727-5276

University of Arkansas at Pine Bluff

1200 N. University Dr.

PO Box 4008

Pine Bluff, AR 71601

Phone: (501) 543-8471

Fax: (501) 543-8003

E-mail: adm@vx4500.uapb.edu

University of the District of Columbia

Office of the Registrar

4200 Connecticut Ave., NW, Bldg.34, Room A-04

Washington, DC 20008

Phone: (202) 274-5100

Fax: (202) 274-5304

- public land-grant university (urban)
- library collection houses over 500,000 volumes and 500 periodicals, microforms, and media resources

University of Maryland - Eastern Shore

Office of Admissions

Princess Anne, MD 21853

Undergraduate admissions: (410) 651-6101

Graduate admissions: (410) 651-6080

E-mail: rpeoples@umes3.umd.edu

E-mail: dignasia@umes-bird.umd.edu

Apply online at: http://www.umes.edu/~home/admissions

The Frederick Douglass Library houses over 170,000 volumes and 1000 periodical subscriptions, with a sizable collection of government documents, CD-ROM databases, and audiovisual materials.

University of the Virgin Islands:

St. Croix Campus

RR-02 Box 10,000

Kingshill, St. Croix,

US Virgin Islands, 00851

Phone: (809) 778-1620

Fax: (809) 693-1005

St. Thomas Campus
2 John Brewer's Bay
St. Thomas
US Virgin Islands 00802
Phone: (809) 693-1000

- public, liberal arts college
- library collection (St. Croix) houses 26,000 books and 325 journals; also contains a CD-ROM lab
- approximately 2610 students (St. Croix)

Virginia State University
PO Box 9001
Petersburg, VA 23806
Phone: (804) 524-5090
Fax: (804) 524-6506

- public, non-sectarian, 4-year university
- library collection houses 280,599 monographs, 1196 periodicals and newspapers, 682,227 microforms, and 81,908 audiovisual materials

Virginia Union University
1500 N. Lombardy St.
Richmond, VA 23220
Phone: (804) 257-5835
Fax: (804) 257-5833

Voorhees College
1411 Voorhees Rd.

Denmark, SC 29042

Phone: (803) 793-3544

Fax: (803) 793-4584

- private, 4-year liberal arts college affiliated with the Episcopal Church
- library collection houses approximately 100,000 volumes of books and periodicals
- approximately 800 undergraduates

West Virginia State University

PO Box 399

Institute, WV 25112

Phone: (304) 766-3111

Fax: (304) 768-9842

Wilberforce University

1055 N. Bickett

Wilberforce, OH 45384

Phone: (513) 376-2911

Fax: (513) 376-5787

Oldest private African-American university in the nation, affiliated with the African Methodist Episcopal Church.

Wiley College

711 Wiley Ave.

Marshall, TX 75670

Phone: (903) 927-3300

Fax: (903) 938-8100

Winston Salem State University

601 M.L.K., Jr. Drive

Winston Salem, NC 27110

Phone: (910) 750-2041

Fax: (910) 750-2049

Xavier University of New Orleans

7325 Palmetto St.

New Orleans, LA 70125

Phone: (504) 483-7541

Fax: (504) 482-2801

E-mail: apply@xula.edu

- private university affiliated with the Catholic Church, founded in 1915 to serve Native and African Americans
- library Resource Center houses over 200,000 titles, 1100 periodical and newspaper subscriptions, and 100,000 microfilms
- over 50% of student body enrolled in natural sciences
- approximately 3500 enrolled
- student/faculty ratio: 14:1

Special Programs

African Studies

Indiana University

Woodburn Hall 221

Bloomington, IN 47405

Phone: (812) 855-6825

Fax: (812) 855-6734

E-mail: afrist@indiana.edu

Director of the African Studies Program: York Bradshaw

Phone: (812) 855-6825

E-mail: bradsha@indiana.edu

Offers an interdisciplinary program in African Studies.

The African Studies Program of The University of Wisconsin at Madison

205 Ingraham Hall

1155 Observatory Dr.

Madison, WI 53706

Phone: (608) 262-2380

Fax: (608) 265-5851

E-mail: AFRST@macc.wisc.edu

The Program offers both graduate and undergraduate students an opportunity to develop a study of Africa through the inclusion of a broad range of disciplines. Concentrations and majors are offered at the undergraduate level, while graduate students may earn a PhD minor or certificate. The Program also includes the Department of African Languages and Literature.

Black World Studies

Loyola University, Chicago

6525 N. Sheridan Rd.

Chicago, IL 60626

Phone: (773) 508-3670

Fax: (773) 508-8797

Internet: http://www.luc.edu/depts/blackworld

E-mail: akarani@luc.edu

Offers a minor *acquainting students with the history of the African American experience in the U.S., Africa and the Caribbean.*

Department of African American Studies
Northwestern University, Evanston Campus
308 Kresge Hall
Evanston, IL 60208-2208
Phone: (847) 491-5122

This program focuses primarily on African-Americans and the African Diaspora in the United States.

Department of Afro-American Studies
Indiana University
Professor John McCluskey, Chairperson
Memorial Hall East - M37
Bloomington, IN 47405
Phone: (812) 855-3875

The Department provides an eclectic analysis of Afro-American heritage and strives to introduce the student to a wide range of current research and scholarly opinion on the history, culture, and social status of Black Americans and their African heritage. The Department offers an undergraduate major and a PhD minor in Afro-American Studies; they also provide a departmental honors program for undergraduates.

The Ohio University African Studies Program
Ohio University - Burson House
56 E. Union
Athens, OH 45701
Phone: (614) 593-1840
Fax: (614) 593-1837
Contact: Dr. W. Stephen Howard, Associate Professor
Phone: (614) 593-1834

E-mail: howards@ouvaxa.cats.ohiou.edu

Offers an MA program in International Affairs with a major in African Studies.

University of South Carolina
African-American Studies
James A. Miller, Director
College of Liberal Arts, 251 Gambrell Hall
Columbia, SC 29208
Phone: (803) 777-7161
Fax: (803) 777-4532
E-mail: millerj@garnet.cla.sc.edu

Offers an interdisciplinary BA in African-American Studies.

University of South Carolina
African Studies
Mark Delancey, Director
College of Liberal Arts
E-mail: delancey@garnet.cla.sc.edu

Offers an interdisciplinary minor in African Studies.

Special Centers

African Studies Center
Boston University
Professor James McCann, Director
James Pritchett, Assistant Director: pritchet@acs.bu.edu
270 Bay State Rd.

Boston, MA 02215

Phone: (617) 353-3673

Established in 1953, the Center was one of the first graduate programs in the U.S. to offer a multidisciplinary African Studies curriculum. It offers a graduate certificate and undergraduate minor in African Studies.

African Studies Center
Michigan State University
100 International Center
E. Lansing, MI 48824-1035
Phone: (517) 353-1700
Fax: (517) 432-1209
Internet: http://www.isp.msu.edu/AfricanStudies
E-mail: Africa@pilot.msu.edu
Assistant Director Yacob Fisseha: fissehay@pilot.msu.edu

The African Studies Center coordinates teaching, research, and public service programs related to Africa throughout the university, and provides programs and services for approximately 200 students from over 30 countries. Through the Center, graduate students may receive a Graduate Certificate (PhD) or Concentration (MA or MS) in African Studies. Undergraduates may receive a Certificate.

The African Studies Center
University of Pennsylvania
Professor Sandra T. Barnes, Director
Room 642, Williams Hall
Phone: (215) 898-6971
E-mail: africa@sas.upenn.edu

The Center is a member of a consortium that includes Haverford, Bryn Mawr, and Swarthmore Colleges; students may take courses for credit at any consortium campus. They offer an interdisciplinary program that gives undergraduate students an opportunity to explore the diversity of sub-Saharan African people and cultures. The Center also offers a certificate program in African Studies for MA and PhD students.

Center for African Studies
The University of Florida
427 Grinter Hall
Gainesville, FL 32611
Phone: (352) 392-2183
Fax: (352) 392-2435

Undergraduates may earn a minor in African Studies, while graduate students may earn either a minor or a certificate. The Center offers an online journal (African Studies Quarterly) and an extensive film collection.

Center for African Studies
University of Illinois at Urbana-Champaign
210 International Studies Bldg.
910 S. 5th St.
Champaign, IL 61820
Phone: (217) 333-6335
Fax: (217) 244-2429

The Center offers a formal minor at the undergraduate level and an interdisciplinary MA degree and PhD minor at the graduate level. They also offer a program in African languages.

Center for Afroamerican and African Studies

University of Michigan, Ann Arbor
200 West Hall Bldg.
Ann Arbor, MI 48109-1092
Phone: (734) 764-5513
E-mail: caasinformation@umich.edu

The Center houses inter-departmental and multidisciplinary programs of study that include historical, sociocultural, psychological, economic, and political approaches and perspective. They offer an academic concentration at the undergraduate level.

Center for African and African-American Studies
The University of Texas at Austin
Jester Center, Room A232A
Austin, TX 78712-1086
Phone: (512) 471-1784
Contact: Dr. Edmund T. Gordon, Program Coordinator
The University of Texas at Austin
Department of Anthropology
E.P. Schoch Building, Room 1.130
Austin, TX 78712-1086
Phone: (512) 471-7537

Created in 1969 in response to the desire of the African-American community in Austin for a program that concentrated on the experience and history of African-Americans, the Center focuses on the African diaspora throughout the world. They offer a BA in African and African-American Studies. They also coordinate the African Diaspora Graduate Program in Anthropology; this program gives special emphasis to the diaspora in the Americas. For more information about the graduate program, contact:

The Institute of African Studies
Columbia University
1103 International Affairs Bldg.
420 W. 118th St.
New York, NY 10027
Phone: (212) 854-4633
Fax: (212) 854-4639
E-mail: african-institute@columbia.edu

The Institute encourages an interdisciplinary approach to research and training. Through the Institute, undergraduates can major or minor in African Studies, while graduate students can complete a regional concentration or a certificate in African Studies in conjunction with an advanced degree from one of Columbia's schools or departments. The certificate requires proficiency in an African language. The Institute also offers a combined program with the Teacher's College, leading to the African certificate and the PhD in education or the EdD degree.

The James S. Coleman African Studies Center
University of California at Los Angeles
10244 Bunche Hall
PO Box 951310
Los Angeles, CA 90095-1310
Phone: (310) 825-3686
Fax: (310) 206-2250
Internet: http://www.isop.ucla.edu/jscasc
E-mail: jscasc@isop.ucla.edu
Hours: 8am-5pm, M-F, except university holidays

The Center offers an MA program in African Area Studies, thus providing graduate students an opportunity to engage in intensive study and research on

Africa on an interdisciplinary basis. They also offer an undergraduate specialization in African Area Studies.

The Race Relations Institute at Fisk University

1000 17th Ave. N.

Nashville, TN 37208-3051

Phone: (615) 329-8575

Fax: (615) 329-8806

E-mail: rwinbush@usit.net

Founded by Dr. Charles S. Johnson in 1942, the Institute has a legacy of promoting justice, freedom, and equality for peoples everywhere who have been victimized by racist discrimination.

The Schomburg Center for Research on Black Culture
New York Public Libraries

515 Malcolm X Blvd.

New York, NY 10037-1801

Phone: (212) 491-2200

Promotes study of the histories and cultures of Africa and of peoples of African descent throughout the world. Comprised of five divisions: Art and Artifacts, General Research and Reference, Manuscripts, Archives and Rare Books, Moving Image and Recorded Sound, and Photographs and Prints. Collections are particularly strong in the arts, humanities, and social sciences. (Amy Bell, 1996)

The Stanford-Berkeley Joint Center for African Studies

Center for African Studies:

Stanford University

342/356 Stephens Hall

Stanford, CA 94305-5013

Phone: (650) 723-0295

Fax: (650) 723-6784

University of California at Berkeley Institute for International Studies

Littlefield Center, Room 14

Berkeley, CA 94720-2314

Phone: (510) 642-8338

Fax: (510) 642-0721

E-mail: asc@uclink.berkeley.edu

The Center coordinates an interdisciplinary program in African Studies for graduate and undergraduate students from various departments. It was established in 1979 as an interdisciplinary research center.

Publishers

African Books Collective, Ltd.

The Jam Factory

27 Park End St.

Oxford OX1 1HU, UK

Phone: +44-(0) 1865-726686

E-mail: abc@dial.pipex.com

Founded in 1989 by 17 African publishers who own the company, the Collective is a source of supply for the English-language titles of 48 African publishers. They currently stock 1700 titles.

National Newspaper Publishers Association

3200 13th St. NW

Washington, DC 20010

Phone: (202) 588-8764

Fax: (202) 588-5029

Internet: www.nnpa.org

Represents approximately 200 of the nation's black newspapers. Their archives are located at Howard University at the Moorland Spingarn Center. Their mission is *to promote the interest of the Black Press by securing unity and action in all matters relative to the profession of journalism and the business of publishing.*

Sage Publications, Inc.

2455 Teller Rd.

Thousand Oaks, CA 91320

Phone: (805) 499-0721

Internet: www.sagepub.com

Sage Publications serves an international community of scholars in social science, science, and electronic publishing.

Quiet Time Publishing

PO Box 10366

Marina del Rey, CA 90295

Phone: (310) 452-2922

Exists to *provide quality books for African Americans.*

Government Programs

Commission on Civil Rights

624 9th Street, NW

Washington, D.C. 20425

Western Regional Office

Suite 810

3660 Wilshire Boulevard

Los Angeles, California 90010

Contact: Philip Montez, Director

Phone: (213) 894-3437

Internet: http://www.usccr.gov

The U.S. Commission on Civil Rights is an independent, bipartisan agency first established by Congress in 1957 and reestablished in 1983. It is directed to:

- *Investigate complaints alleging that citizens are being deprived of their right to vote by reason of their race, color, religion, sex, age, disability, or national origin, or by reason of fraudulent practices;*

- *Study and collect information relating to discrimination or a denial of equal protection of the laws under the Constitution because of race, color, religion, sex, age, disability, or national origin, or in the administration of justice;*

- *Appraise Federal laws and policies with respect to discrimination or denial of equal protection of the laws because of race, color, religion, sex, age, disability, or national origin, or in the administration of justice;*

- *Serve as a national clearinghouse for information in respect to discrimination or denial of equal protection of the laws because of race, color, religion, sex, age, disability, or national origin;*

- *Submit reports, findings, and recommendations to the President and Congress;*

- *Issue public service announcements to discourage discrimination or denial of equal protection of the laws.*

Department of Commerce
Census Bureau
American Fact Finder

Internet: http://factfinder.census.gov/java_prod/dads.ui.homePage.HomePage

Provides information from 1990 census in variety of forms. Allows the user to create profiles of almost any American community or region based on demographics data such as income and more.

Minority Business Development Agency
14th St. & Constitution Ave., NW

Room 5055

Washington, DC 20230

Internet: http://www.mbda.gov

Feedback Form: http://www.mbda.gov/contact.asp

The Minority Business Development Agency (MBDA), is part of the U.S. Department of Commerce. MBDA is the only Federal Agency created specifically to foster the creation, growth and expansion of minority-owned businesses in America.

Department of Education
Office for Civil Rights
Customer Service Team

Mary E. Switzer Building

330 C Street, SW

Washington, DC 20202

Phone: (202) 205-5413; 1-800-421-3481

Fax: (202) 205-9862

Internet: http://www.ed.gov/offices/OCR

E-mail: OCR@ED.Gov

Assistant Secretary Office of Civil Rights: Norma V. Cantu

The mission of the Office for Civil Rights is to ensure equal access to education and to promote educational excellence throughout the nation through vigorous enforcement of civil rights. A primary responsibility is resolving complaints of discrimination. Agency-initiated cases, typically called compliance reviews, permit OCR to target resources on compliance problems that appear particularly acute. OCR also provides technical assistance to help institutions achieve voluntary compliance with the civil rights laws that OCR enforces. In addition, OCR provides support to other Department of Education programs.

Office of Educational Research and Improvement (OERI)

U.S. Department of Education

OERI/At-Risk Room 610

555 New Jersey Avenue, NW

Washington, DC 20208-5521

Phone: (202) 219-2239

Fax: (202) 219-2030

Internet: http://www.ed.gov/offices/OERI/At-Risk

Contact: Holly Martinez, Acting Director

Phone: (202) 219-2239

E-mail: Debra_Hollinger_Martinez@ed.gov

The National Institute on the Education of At-Risk Students (At-Risk Institute) is one of five Institutes created by the Educational Research, Development, Dissemination and Improvement Act of 1994. These Institutes are located within the Office of Educational Research and Improvement at the U.S. Department of Education. The At-Risk Institute supports a range of research and development activities designed to improve the education of students at risk of educational failure because of limited English proficiency, poverty, race, geographic location, or economic disadvantage.

Department of Health and Human Services
Centers for Disease Control and Prevention
Office of the Director
Associate Director for Minority Health

Walter Williams, Associate Director, Minority Health
Phone: 404-639-7210
Contact: Corlis Voltz
E-mail: cav2@cdc.gov
Internet: http://www.cdc.gov/od/admh

The mission of the Office of the Associate Director for Minority Health is to improve the health of the African-American (Blacks, Asian-American/Pacific Islander, Hispanic American, and Native American/Alaska Native Citizens, and, where appropriate, similar ethnic/racial subgroups both in and out of the United States, through policy development and program analysis at CDC and ATSDR.

National Institutes of Health
NIH Office of Extramural Research
Minorities Training Programs

Internet: http://grants.nih.gov/training/minorities.htm

Offers links to organizations that offer grant money for minority-based research.

Department of Housing and Urban Development
Headquarters Program Office
Office of Fair Housing and Equal Opportunity

US Department of Housing and Urban Development

451 7th Street SW

Washington, DC 20410

Phone: (202) 401-0388 (HUD)

Internet: http://www.hud.gov/fhe/fheo.html

Contact: N. Mykl Asanti

E-mail: N._Mykl_Asanti@hud.gov

This office exists to *enforce the Fair Housing Act and other civil rights laws to ensure the right of equal housing opportunity and free and fair housing choice without discrimination based on race, color, religion, sex, national origin, disability or family composition.* Its stated goals are to:

1. *Reduce discrimination in housing by doubling the Title VIII case load by the end of 2000 through aggressive enforcement of civil rights and fair housing laws;*

2. *Promote geographic mobility for low-income and minority households;*

3. *Integrate fair housing plans into HUD's Consolidated Plans;*

4. *Further fair housing in other relevant programs of the Federal government; and*

5. *Promote substantial equivalency among state, local and community organizations involved in providing housing.*

Department of Justice
Office of General Council
Civil Rights Division

Office of the Assistant Attorney General

Acting Director: Bill Lann Lee

P.O. Box 65808

Washington, D.C. 20035-5808

Phone: (202) 514-4609

Fax: (202) 514-0293

            (202) 307-2572

(202) 307-2839

Internet: http://www.usdoj.gov/crt/crt-home.html

The Civil Rights Division has served for the past 40 years as the federal government's chief guardian of the right of each and every person to live, learn, and work free from discrimination and threat of harm. The civil rights laws of the United States prohibit discrimination based on a number of factors -- including race, color, religion, sex, national origin, disability, age, familial status, citizenship status, marital status, and source of income -- in employment, education, public accommodations, housing, lending, programs receiving federal financial assistance, and in other areas.

Department of State and Institute of International Education
Fulbright Program

IIE

809 United Nations Plaza

New York, NY 10017-3580

Internet: http://www.iie.org/fulbright

The Fulbright Program was established in 1946, at the end of World War II, to increase mutual understanding between the people of the United States and other countries, through the exchange of persons, knowledge, and skills. Grants are made to citizens of participating countries, primarily for:

- *university teaching;*
- *advanced research;*
- *graduate study; and*
- *teaching in elementary and secondary schools.*

Office of Undersecretary for Public Diplomacy and Public Affairs

Public Information, Rm. 6808

Bureau of Public Affairs

U.S. Department of State

Washington, DC 20520-6810

Phone: (202) 647-6575

(use this address for the bureaus listed below)

Office of International Information Programs
Office of Geographic Liaison
Bureau of African Affairs

Phone: (202) 647-7371

Internet: http://www.state.gov/www/regions/africa/index.html

The Bureau of African Affairs, headed by Assistant Secretary of State Susan E. Rice, advises the Secretary and guides the operation of the U.S. diplomatic establishment in the countries of Sub-Saharan Africa.

Bureau of Western Hemisphere Affairs

Internet: http://www.state.gov/www/regions/ara/index.html

The Bureau of Western Hemisphere Affairs, headed by Acting Assistant Secretary of State Peter F. Romero, is responsible for managing and promoting U.S. interests in the region by supporting democracy, trade, and sustainable economic development, and fostering cooperation on issues such as drug trafficking and crime, poverty reduction, and environmental protection.

Bureau of Educational and Cultural Affairs

Internet: http://e.usia.gov/education

The Bureau of Educational and Cultural Affairs (ECA) fosters mutual understanding between the United States and other countries through international educational and training programs. The bureau does so by promoting personal, professional, and institutional ties between private citizens

and organizations in the United States and abroad, as well as by presenting U.S. history, society, art and culture in all of its diversity to overseas audiences.

Environmental Protection Agency
Office of Civil Rights

1200 Pennsylvania Avenue, NW

Washington, DC 20004

Phone: (202) 260-4575

Fax: (202) 260-4580

Internet: http://www.epa.gov (EPA home)

Works to ensure, among other things, compliance with civil rights laws by recipients of EPA funds.

Equal Employment Opportunity Commission

1801 L Street, NW

Washington, DC 20507

Phone: (202) 663-4900

Internet: http://www.eeoc.gov

Chairwoman: Ida A. Castro

Enforces civil rights laws as they pertain to hiring practices and workplace environment. The mission of the EEOC, as set forth in its strategic plan, is to promote equal opportunity in employment through administrative and judicial enforcement of the federal civil rights laws and through education and technical assistance.

Library of Congress
Reading Rooms

101 Independence Ave. SE

Washington, DC 20540

Phone: (202) 707-5000 or (202) 707-6500 (researchers' information)

Internet: http://lcweb.loc.gov/rr

Archives of various data, including African and Middle Eastern, Asian and genealogy.

Smithsonian Institution
> **National Museum of African Art**

950 Independence Avenue, SW

Washington, DC

Phone: (202) 357-4600

Fax: (202) 357-4879

Internet: http://www.si.edu/organiza/museums/africart/start.htm

Director: Dr. Roslyn A. Walker

Seeks to create a greater understanding of the visual art of Africa, both ancient and modern. Supports research and public programs.

Journals

African American Review

African Studies Quarterly

Internet: http://web.africa.ufl.edu/asq/index.htm

E-mail: asq@africa.ufl.edu

The University of Florida's peer-reviewed, interdisciplinary on-line journal.

Black Child

Interrace Publications

2870 Peachtree Rd., Ste.264

Atlanta, GA 30355

Phone: (404) 633-9234

Black Child Advocate

National Black Child Development Institute

1023 15th St. NW, 6th floor

Washington, DC 20005

Black Family

Family Publication, Inc.

PO Box 1046

Herndon, VA 22070-1046

Black Health

Black Health, Inc.

PO Box 5276

FDR Station

New York, NY 10150-5276

Black Renaissance/Renaissance Noire

Journals Division - Indiana University Press

601 N. Morton St.

Bloomington, IN 47404

Phone: 1-800-842-6796 or (812) 855-9449

Named one of the ten best magazines of 1996 by Library Journal, this journal aims to "bring the voices of black intellectuals to a wider audience." Publishes essays, fiction, reviews, and art work.

Callaloo

Ethnicity and Disease
2045 Manchester St. NW
Atlanta, GA 30324-4110
Phone: (404) 875-6263

Journal of African American Men
Transaction Publication
Transition Periodicals Consortium
Dept.3092
Rutgers University
New Brunswick, NJ 08903

Journal of Aging and Ethnicity
Springer Publishing Co.
536 Broadway
New York, NY 10012-3955

Journal of the Association of Academic Minority Physicians
Office of the Secretary
University of Maryland - School of Medicine
655 W. Baltimore St.
Baltimore, MD 21201
Phone: (410) 706-3100
Internet: www.ab.umd.edu

Journal of Black Psychology
Sage Publications, Inc.
2455 Teller Rd.
Thousand Oaks, CA 91320
Phone: (805) 499-0721
Internet: www.sagepub.com

Journal of Black Studies

Journal of Blacks in Higher Education

Journal for Minority Medical Students
Spectrum Unlimited
4203 Canal St.
New Orleans, LA 70019
Phone: (504) 488-5100
Internet: http://www.gnofn.org/~spectrum

Journal of the National Black Nurses Association
1511 K St. NW, Ste.415
Washington, DC 20005

Journal of Negro Education

Journal of Negro History

Souls
Columbia University

Studies in African Linguistics
Robert Botne, editor

Department of Linguistics

Memorial Hall 322

Indiana University

Bloomington, IN 47405

Information about subscriptions and publication can be obtained through the African Studies Program (under *Special Programs*).

Western Journal of Black Studies

subscription info: WJBS

Washington State University Press

Cooper Publications Bldg.

Pullman, WA 99164-5910

manuscript info: E. Lincoln Jones, editor

WJBS

Cleveland Hall 57-P, Washington State Univ.

Pullman, WA 99164-8681

Phone: (509) 335-8681

E-mail: wjbs@wsunix.wsu.edu

Recently awarded the C.L.R. James Award for promoting outstanding scholarship regarding African-American issues, this interdisciplinary quarterly deals with research, social analysis, political commentary, and contemporary arts as they pertain to the African and African-American experience.

II. Asian-Americans

Libraries and Archival Resources

American Oriental Society Library
Sterling Memorial Library, Room 329
Yale University
New Haven, CT 06520

Asian-American Studies Library
Ethnic Studies Library
The University of California - Berkeley
3407 Dwinelle Hall
Berkeley, CA 94720
Phone: (510) 642-2220
Internet: http://eslibrary.berkeley.edu/aaslhome.html
E-mail: wcpoon@library.berkeley.edu
Contact: Mrs. Wei Chi Poon

Houses 52,000 holdings, including 20,000 archive materials, 11,800 monographs, and 216 serials. Contains materials relevant to the experience of Asian, Chinese, Japanese, Korean, Filipino, Asian Indian and Southeast Asian Americans.

Asian Community Library
Oakland Public Library
125 14th St.
Oakland, CA 94612

East Asian Library - The University of California at Berkeley
208 Durant Hall
Berkeley, CA 94720-6000

Phone: (510) 642-2556

Fax: (510) 642-3817

Houses a comprehensive research collection of materials in Chinese, Japanese, Korean, Manchu, Mongolian, and Tibetan. Stocks, except for Rare Book titles, are open to all users. Much of the collection may be borrowed for use outside of the Library. (East Asian Library)

California Institute of Asian Studies - Library

3494 21st St.

San Francisco, CA 94110

Chinese Cultural Center - Library

159 Lexington Ave.

New York, NY 10016

East Asian Collection

Ohio State University

1858 Nei Ave.

Columbus, OH 43210

Library of Congress - Asian Division

John Adams Bldg., Room 1024

Washington, DC 20540

Popular Media

A Magazine

phone: 1-800-446-6233

Internet: http://www.amagazine.com

The largest publication for English-speaking Asians in America

Asian American Resources (MIT)
Internet: http://www.mit.edu/activities/aar/aar.html

According to InfoSurf's Asian-American Studies Web Page, *the most comprehensive site for Asian-American Resources.*

Asian Voices
Phone: (212) 998-4942

The annual publication of the Asian Cultural Union at New York University, this magazine allows Asian students to express their ideas and opinions. All Asian-related topics are welcome for submission.

AsianWeek
Internet: http://www.asianweek.com

Online news magazine focusing on current events in Asian countries.

Filipinas Magazine
363 El Camino Real, Suite 100
South San Francisco, CA 94080
Phone: (650) 872-8650
Fax: (650) 872-8651
Internet: http://www.filipinasmag.com

The Filipino Express Newspaper and Online Magazine
2711 Kennedy Blvd.
Jersey City, NJ 07306

Phone: (201) 434-1114

Fax: (201) 434-0880

Internet: http://www.filipinoexpress.com

E-mail: Filexpress@aol.com

Rated four stars by NetGuide magazine, this online magazine covers news, arts and entertainment relevant to the Filipino American community.

Orient Magazine

PO Box 150067

Altamonte Springs, FL 32715-0067

Phone: (407) 831-0083

Fax: (407) 831-0073

Internet: http://www.orientmag.com/contact.htm

Celebrating the Asian American experience.

Pakistan Link

10564 Progress Way, Suite D

Cypress, CA 90630

Phone: (714) 236-7910

Fax: (714) 236-7911

Internet: http://www.pakistanlink.com/

Editor In Chief: M. Faiz Rehman

The largest Pakistani-American newspaper and the first Pakistani newspaper on the Internet, since 1994.

Pakistan Today Magazine

13949 Seville Ave.

Fontana, CA 92335

Phone: (909) 350-0358

Fax: (909) 350-0359

Internet: http://www.paktoday.com

E-mail: mail@paktoday.com

Editor In Chief: Tashbih Sayyed

Winner of The "Best of Pakistan" Award.

Philippine News Link

PO Box 20334

El Sobrante, CA 94803-0334

Internet: http://www.datu.com/main.htm

E-mail: webmaster@philnews.com

Focuses on different provinces of the country.

Time.com/Asia Magazine

Time magazine, with Asia as its focus.

Yolk Magazine

PO Box 862130

Los Angeles, CA 90086-2130

Message line: (310) 917-7252

Fax: (213) 223-7900

Internet: info@YOLK.com

Office hours: 9:00am - 6:00 pm (PST), weekdays

Electronic magazine about Asian-American pop culture

Colleges/Universities and Special Programs

Asian American Studies
California State University, Northridge
Sierra Hall 103
18111 Nordhoff St.
Northridge, CA 91330
Phone: (818) 677-4966
Fax: (818) 677-7094
Internet: http://www.csun.edu/~hfaas002/aas.html
E-mail: aas.webb@csun.edu
Contact: Liza Kraay

Offers minor in Asian American Studies. BA and MA programs are projected for the future.

Asian Studies
Carleton College
Internet: http://www.carleton.edu/curricular/ASST/index.html

Concentrates on East Asian and South Asian civilizations. Offers a major and concentration in Asian Studies.

Asian and Asian American Studies Program
Center for Interdisciplinary Studies
Loyola University, Chicago
Lake Shore Campus, Damen Hall 105
6525 N. Sheridan Rd.
Chicago, IL 60626
Phone: (773) 508-2935
Fax: (773) 508-8797

Internet: http://www.luc.edu/depts/asian_st

Director: Dr. Yvonne Lau

Offers minor in Asian and Asian American Studies.

Asian American Studies Program
University of Massachusetts, Boston

100 Morrissey Blvd.

Boston, MA 02125-3393

Phone: (617) 287-7614

Fax: (617) 287-5656

Internet: http://omega.cc.umb.edu/~aast/main.html

Asian American Studies Program
Pitzer College

1050 N. Mills Ave.

Claremont, CA 91711

Internet: http://www.pitzer.edu/~lyamane/amajor.htm

E-mail: lyamane@calvin.pitzer.edu

- offers a BA major
- open to all students of The Claremont Colleges.

Asian American Studies Program
University of Wisconsin – Madison

303 Ingraham Hall

1155 Observatory Dr.

Madison, WI 53706

Phone: (608) 263-2976

Fax: (608) 265-8110

E-mail: hgshah@facstaff.wisc.edu

Director: Hemant Shah

Offers a Certificate in Asian American Studies to graduates. A major is projected in the future.

East Asia Program
Cornell University
140 Uris Hall
Ithaca, NY 14853-7601
Phone: (607) 255-6222
Fax: (607) 255-1388
Internet: http://www.einaudi.cornell.edu/Eastasia/
E-mail: cueap@cornell.edu

East Asian Studies Program
George Washington University
Elliot School of International Affairs
Director: Bruce J. Dickson
Internet: http://www.gwu.edu/~eastasia/

- offers a BA and MA in East Asian Studies
- graduate certificate in Chinese and East Asian Studies.

East Asian Studies Program
University of Wisconsin – Madison
330 Ingraham Hall
Madison, WI 53706
Phone: (608) 262-3643
Fax: (608) 265-2919
Internet: http://polyglot.lss.wisc.edu/east/eas.html
E-mail: eas@macc.wisc.edu

Devoted to the study of China, Japan and Korea. Offers an undergraduate major.

South Asia Program
Cornell University
170 Uris Hall
Ithaca, NY 14853-7601
Internet: http://www.einaudi.cornell.edu/SouthAsia/

Focuses on the Indian subcontinent. Offers an undergraduate concentration in South Asia Studies and a Master's Degree in Asian Studies with a concentration in South Asia Studies.

Southeast Asia Program
Cornell University
180 Uris Hall
Ithaca, NY 14853
Phone: (607) 255-2378
Fax: (607) 254-5000
Internet: http://www.einaudi.cornell.edu/SouthEastAsia/
E-mail: SEAP@cornell.edu

Offers graduate specialization in Southeast Asian Studies.

Special Centers

Center for South Asia
University of Wisconsin, Madison
203 Ingraham Hall
1155 Observatory Dr.

Madison, WI 53706

Phone: (608) 262-4884

Fax: (608) 265-3062

Internet: http://www.wisc.edu/southasia/

E-mail: sasianctr@macc.wisc.edu

Provides access to resources for teaching about South Asia [particularly India, Pakistan, Nepal and Tibet] *at the K-12, secondary, and post-secondary level, and to the community at large.*

Center for Southeast Asian Studies
University of Wisconsin, Madison
207 Ingraham Hall

1155 Observatory Dr.

Madison, WI 53706

Phone: (608) 263-1755

Fax: (608) 263-3735

Internet: http://www.wisc.edu/ctrseasia

E-mail: seasian@macc.wisc.edu

Institute for Asian American Studies
University of Massachusetts, Boston
Healey Library 10-7

100 Morrissey Blvd.

Boston, MA 02125-3393

Phone: (617) 287-5650

Fax: (617) 287-5656

Established in 1993, *The Institute brings together resources and expertise within both the university and the community to conduct research on Asian Americans;*

to expand Asian American studies in the curriculum; and to strengthen the community development capacity of Asian Americans.

Sigur Center for Asian Studies
George Washington University
Stuart Hall
2013 G Street, NW, Suite 301
Washington, DC 20052
Director: Bruce Dickson
Phone: (202) 994-5886
Fax: (202) 994-6096
Internet: http://www.gwu.edu/~sigur/
E-mail: sigur@www.gwu.edu

An international research center of The Elliott School of International Affairs at GWU.

South Asia Center
Syracuse University
346G Eggers Hall
The Maxwell School
Syracuse, NY 13244
Director: Susan S. Wadley
Phone: (315) 443-2553
Fax: (315) 443-9085
Internet: http://www.maxwell.syr.edu/gai/south-asia-center/
E-mail: southasia@maxwell.syr.edu

Administers an undergraduate minor and a graduate certificate program. Coordinates colloquia, films, cultural programs and other activities.

The University of Arizona Asian Pacific American Cultural/Resource Center

The University of Arizona, MLK Bldg., Room 320

PO Box 210128

Tucson, AZ 85721-0128

Phone: (520) 621-3481

Fax: (520) 621-7574

E-mail: apasc@w3.arizona.edu

Hours: M-Th 8:30-5:30, Friday 8:30-4:00

Provides library resources, a newsletter, advising, workshops, and literature. Houses the Asian-American Cultural Association and the Hawaii Club.

The University of California, Los Angeles (UCLA) Asian American Studies Center

3230 Campbell Hall

405 Hilgard Ave.

Los Angeles, CA 90095-1546

Phone: (310) 825-2974

Fax: (310) 206-9844

Internet: http://www.sscnet.ucla.edu/aasc

E-mail: dtn@ucla.edu

Offers an MA in Asian American Studies and Public Health, and a minor in Asian American Studies. Also publishes the Amerasia Journal.

Publishers

Alta Mira Press

1630 N. Main St., Ste.367

Walnut Creek, CA 94596

Phone: (510) 938-7243

Fax: (510) 933-9720

E-mail: explore@altamira.sagepub.com

Alta Mira puts out numerous publications in the categories of Asian Pacific American Studies and South Asian Studies.

Government Programs

Agency for International Development

Ronald Reagan Building

Washington, DC 20523-1000

Phone: (202) 712-4810

Fax: (202) 216-3524

Internet: http://www.info.usaid.gov

Federal agency that effects international aid programs in order *to advance the political and economic interests of the United States.*

Commission on Civil Rights

624 9th Street, NW

Washington, D.C. 20425

Western Regional Office

Suite 810

3660 Wilshire Boulevard

Los Angeles, California 90010

Contact: Philip Montez, Director

Phone: (213) 894-3437

Internet: http://www.usccr.gov

The U.S. Commission on Civil Rights is an independent, bipartisan agency first established by Congress in 1957 and reestablished in 1983. It is directed to:

- *Investigate complaints alleging that citizens are being deprived of their right to vote by reason of their race, color, religion, sex, age, disability, or national origin, or by reason of fraudulent practices;*
- *Study and collect information relating to discrimination or a denial of equal protection of the laws under the Constitution because of race, color, religion, sex, age, disability, or national origin, or in the administration of justice;*
- *Appraise Federal laws and policies with respect to discrimination or denial of equal protection of the laws because of race, color, religion, sex, age, disability, or national origin, or in the administration of justice;*
- *Serve as a national clearinghouse for information in respect to discrimination or denial of equal protection of the laws because of race, color, religion, sex, age, disability, or national origin;*
- *Submit reports, findings, and recommendations to the President and Congress;*
- *Issue public service announcements to discourage discrimination or denial of equal protection of the laws.*

Department of Commerce
Census Bureau

American Fact Finder

Internet: http://factfinder.census.gov/java_prod/dads.ui.homePage.HomePage

Provides information from 1990 census in variety of forms. Allows the user to create profiles of almost any American community or region based on demographics data such as income and more.

Minority Business Development Agency

14th St. & Constitution Ave., NW

Room 5055

Washington, DC 20230

Internet: http://www.mbda.gov

Feedback Form: http://www.mbda.gov/contact.asp

The Minority Business Development Agency (MBDA), is part of the U.S. Department of Commerce. MBDA is the only Federal Agency created specifically to foster the creation, growth and expansion of minority-owned businesses in America.

Department of Education

Office of Bilingual Education and Minority Languages Affairs

600 Independence Avenue, SW

Washington, DC 20202-6510

Internet: http://www.ed.gov/offices/OBEMLA

E-mail: askncbe@ncbe.gwu.edu

Contact: Art Love, Acting Director

Phone: (202) 205-5463

E-mail: art_love@ed.gov

Congress passed the Bilingual Education Act in 1968 in recognition of the growing number of linguistically and culturally diverse children enrolled in schools who, because of their limited English proficiency, were not receiving an education equal to their English-proficient peers. The purpose of this Act was, and continues to be, aligned with Title VI of the Civil Rights Act of 1964 which the Department interprets as follows:

Where inability to speak and understand the English language excludes national origin minority group children from effective participation in the educational program offered by a school district, the district must take affirmative steps to rectify the language deficiency in order to open its instructional program to these students.

Established in 1974 by Congress, the Office of Bilingual Education and Minority Languages Affairs helps school districts meet their responsibility to provide equal education opportunity to limited English proficient children.

Office for Civil Rights

Customer Service Team

Mary E. Switzer Building

330 C Street, SW

Washington, DC 20202

Phone: (202) 205-5413; 1-800-421-3481

Fax: (202) 205-9862

Internet: http://www.ed.gov/offices/OCR

E-mail: OCR@ED.Gov

Assistant Secretary Office of Civil Rights: Norma V. Cantu

The mission of the Office for Civil Rights is to ensure equal access to education and to promote educational excellence throughout the nation through vigorous enforcement of civil rights. A primary responsibility is resolving complaints of discrimination. Agency-initiated cases, typically called compliance reviews, permit OCR to target resources on compliance problems that appear particularly acute. OCR also provides technical assistance to help institutions achieve voluntary compliance with the civil rights laws that OCR enforces. In addition, OCR provides support to other Department of Education programs.

Office of Educational Research and Improvement (OERI)

U.S. Department of Education

OERI/At-Risk Room 610

555 New Jersey Avenue, NW

Washington, DC 20208-5521

Phone: (202) 219-2239

Fax: (202) 219-2030

Internet: http://www.ed.gov/offices/OERI/At-Risk

Contact: Holly Martinez, Acting Director

Phone: (202) 219-2239

E-mail: Debra_Hollinger_Martinez@ed.gov

The National Institute on the Education of At-Risk Students (At-Risk Institute) is one of five Institutes created by the Educational Research, Development, Dissemination and Improvement Act of 1994. These Institutes are located within the Office of Educational Research and Improvement at the U.S. Department of Education. The At-Risk Institute supports a range of research and development activities designed to improve the education of students at risk of educational failure because of limited English proficiency, poverty, race, geographic location, or economic disadvantage.

Department of Health and Human Services
Centers for Disease Control and Prevention
Office of the Director
Associate Director for Minority Health

Walter Williams, Associate Director, Minority Health

Phone: 404-639-7210

Contact: Corlis Voltz

E-mail: cav2@cdc.gov

Internet: http://www.cdc.gov/od/admh

The mission of the Office of the Associate Director for Minority Health is to improve the health of the African-American (Blacks, Asian-American/Pacific Islander, Hispanic American, and Native American/Alaska Native Citizens, and, where appropriate, similar ethnic/racial subgroups both in and out of the United States, through policy development and program analysis at CDC and ATSDR.

Department of Housing and Urban Development
Headquarters Program Office
Office of Fair Housing and Equal Opportunity

US Department of Housing and Urban Development

451 7th Street SW

Washington, DC 20410

Phone: (202) 401-0388 (HUD)

Internet: http://www.hud.gov/fhe/fheo.html

Contact: N. Mykl Asanti

E-mail: N._Mykl_Asanti@hud.gov

This office exists to *enforce the Fair Housing Act and other civil rights laws to ensure the right of equal housing opportunity and free and fair housing choice without discrimination based on race, color, religion, sex, national origin, disability or family composition.* Its stated goals are to:

1. *Reduce discrimination in housing by doubling the Title VIII case load by the end of 2000 through aggressive enforcement of civil rights and fair housing laws;*

2. *Promote geographic mobility for low-income and minority households;*

3. *Integrate fair housing plans into HUD's Consolidated Plans;*

4. *Further fair housing in other relevant programs of the Federal government; and*

5. *Promote substantial equivalency among state, local and community organizations involved in providing housing.*

Department of Justice
Office of General Council
Civil Rights Division

Office of the Assistant Attorney General

Acting Director: Bill Lann Lee

P.O. Box 65808

Washington, D.C. 20035-5808

Phone: (202) 514-4609

Fax: (202) 514-0293

      (202) 307-2572

      (202) 307-2839

Internet: http://www.usdoj.gov/crt/crt-home.html

The Civil Rights Division has served for the past 40 years as the federal government's chief guardian of the right of each and every person to live, learn, and work free from discrimination and threat of harm. The civil rights laws of the United States prohibit discrimination based on a number of factors -- including race, color, religion, sex, national origin, disability, age, familial status, citizenship status, marital status, and source of income -- in employment, education, public accommodations, housing, lending, programs receiving federal financial assistance, and in other areas.

Executive Office for Immigration Review

Public Affairs Office

5107 Leesburg Pike, Suite 2400

Falls Church, VA 22041

Phone: (703) 305-0289

Fax: (703) 605-0365

Internet: http://www.usdoj.gov/eoir

Under delegated authority of the Attorney General of the United States, EOIR administers and interprets Federal immigration laws and regulations through the conduct of immigration court proceedings, appellate reviews, and administrative hearings in individual cases. EOIR carries out these responsibilities through its three main components:

1. The Board of Immigration Appeals (BIA), which hears appeals of decisions made in individual cases by Immigration Judges, INS District Directors, or other immigration officials;

2. *The Office of the Chief Immigration Judge (OCIJ), which oversees all the Immigration Courts and their proceedings throughout the United States; and*

3. *The Office of the Chief Administrative Hearing Officer (OCAHO), which became part of EOIR in 1987 to resolve cases concerning employer sanctions, document fraud, and immigration-related employment discrimination.*

The purpose of these proceedings is to provide a process through which individuals can defend themselves against Government charges, complaints, or denials of benefits; or through which they can seek relief from penalties imposed against them. Every proceeding adheres to statutory and regulatory guidelines ensuring the uniform application of law and the fair and equitable treatment of all parties involved.

Office of Immigration
U.S. Immigration and Naturalization Service

425 I St., NW

Washington, DC 20536

Phone: (202) 514-4316

Contact: Commissioner Doris Meissner

Provides service and information to the general public while concurrently exercising its enforcement responsibilities.

Department of State and Institute of International Education
Fulbright Program

IIE

809 United Nations Plaza

New York, NY 10017-3580

Internet: http://www.iie.org/fulbright

The Fulbright Program was established in 1946, at the end of World War II, to increase mutual understanding between the people of the United States and other countries, through the exchange of persons, knowledge, and skills. Grants are made to citizens of participating countries, primarily for:

- *university teaching;*
- *advanced research;*
- *graduate study; and*
- *teaching in elementary and secondary schools*

Office of Undersecretary for Public Diplomacy and Public Affairs

Public Information, Rm. 6808

Bureau of Public Affairs

U.S. Department of State

Washington, DC 20520-6810

Phone: (202) 647-6575

(use this address for the bureaus listed below)

Bureau of East Asian and Pacific Affairs

Internet: http://www.state.gov/www/regions/eap/index.html

The Bureau of East Asian and Pacific Affairs, headed by Assistant Secretary Stanley Roth, deals with U.S. foreign policy and U.S. relations with the countries in the Asia-Pacific region.

Bureau of South Asian Affairs

Phones: Office of India, Nepal and Sri Lanka: (202) 647-2141

Office of Pakistan, Afghanistan and Bangladesh: (202) 647-9552

Office of Regional Affairs: (202) 736-4255

Internet: http://www.state.gov/www/regions/sa/index.html

The Bureau of South Asian Affairs, headed by Assistant Secretary Karl F. Inderfurth, deals with U.S. foreign policy and U.S. relations with the countries in the South Asian region.

Bureau of Educational and Cultural Affairs

Internet: http://e.usia.gov/education

The Bureau of Educational and Cultural Affairs (ECA) fosters mutual understanding between the United States and other countries through international educational and training programs. The bureau does so by promoting personal, professional, and institutional ties between private citizens and organizations in the United States and abroad, as well as by presenting U.S. history, society, art and culture in all of its diversity to overseas audiences.

Office of Undersecretary for Global Affairs
Bureau of Human Rights, Democracy, and Labor

Internet: http://www.state.gov/www/global/human_rights/index.html

This section of the DOS monitors human rights in other countries.

Bureau of Population, Refugees, and Migration

U.S. Department of State

2401 E Street, NW, Suite L-505, SA-1

Washington, D.C. 20522-0105

Internet: http://www.state.gov/www/global/prm/index.html

E-mail: prm@state.gov

Within the government, PRM has primary responsibility for formulating policies on population, refugees, and migration, and for administering U.S. refugee assistance and admissions programs. The Bureau is headed by Assistant Secretary of State Julia V. Taft, under the direction of the Under Secretary of State for Global Affairs.

With a $670 million budget, PRM administers and monitors U.S. contributions to international and non-governmental organizations to assist and protect refugees abroad. In overseeing admissions of refugees to the United States for permanent resettlement, the Bureau works closely with the Immigration and Naturalization Service, the Department of Health and Human Services, and various state and private voluntary agencies.

PRM coordinates U.S. international population policy and promotes its goals through bilateral and multilateral cooperation. It works closely with the U.S. Agency for International Development, which administers U.S. international population programs. The Bureau also coordinates U.S. international migration policy within the U.S. Government and through bilateral and multilateral diplomacy.

Environmental Protection Agency
Office of Civil Rights

1200 Pennsylvania Avenue, NW

Washington, DC 20004

Phone: (202) 260-4575

Fax: (202) 260-4580

Internet: http://www.epa.gov (EPA home)

Works to ensure, among other things, compliance with civil rights laws by recipients of EPA funds.

Equal Employment Opportunity Commission

1801 L Street, NW

Washington, DC 20507

Phone: (202) 663-4900

Internet: http://www.eeoc.gov

Chairwoman: Ida A. Castro

Enforces civil rights laws as they pertain to hiring practices and workplace environment. The mission of the EEOC, as set forth in its strategic plan, is to promote equal opportunity in employment through administrative and judicial enforcement of the federal civil rights laws and through education and technical assistance.

The Japan-U.S. Friendship Commission

1120 Vermont Ave., NW, Room 925

Washington, DC 20005

Phone: (202) 275-7712

Fax: (202) 275-7413

E-mail: 72133.2433@compuserve.com

Independent Federal agency dedicated to promoting cultural understanding and cooperation between the U.S. and Japan.

Library of Congress
Reading Rooms

101 Independence Ave. SE

Washington, DC 20540

Phone: (202) 707-5000 or (202) 707-6500 (researchers' information)

Internet: http://lcweb.loc.gov/rr

Archives of various data, including African and Middle Eastern, Asian and genealogy.

National Institutes of Health

    NIH Office of Extramural Research

Minorities Training Programs

Internet: http://grants.nih.gov/training/minorities.htm

Offers links to organizations that offer grant money for minority-based research.

Journals

Asian American Policy Review

Harvard University

Phone: (617) 496-8635

Fax: (617) 496-9027

Internet: http://www.ksg.harvard.edu/~aapr

E-mail: aapr@harvard.edu

The first academic journal in the country dedicated solely to examining the social issues and public policies affecting the Asian Pacific American community.

China Journal

Ethnicity and Disease

2045 Manchester St., NW

Atlanta, GA 30324-4110

Phone: (404) 875-6263

Harvard Journal of Asiatic Studies

Journal of Aging and Ethnicity

Springer Publishing Co.
536 Broadway
New York, NY 10012-3955

Journal of Asian Studies

Journal of Asian American Studies
Dept. of History
Columbia University
New York, NY 10027
Internet: http://muse.jhu.edu/journals/jaas/information/guidelines.html
Contact: Gary Y. Okihiro

Journal of the Association of Academic Minority Physicians
Office of the Secretary
University of Maryland - School of Medicine
655 W. Baltimore St.
Baltimore, MD 21201
Phone: (410) 706-3100
Internet: www.ab.umd.edu

Journal for Minority Medical Students
Spectrum Unlimited
4203 Canal St.
New Orleans, LA 70019
Phone: (504) 488-5100
Internet: http://www.gnofn.org/~spectrum

Monumenta Nipponica

Pacific Affairs

Sangam (Columbia University's South Asian Journal)

E-mail: sangam@columbia.edu

III. Hawaii and American Samoa

Libraries and Archival Resources

Bishop Museum Library
Bishop Museum – The State Museum of Natural and Cultural History
1525 Bernice St.
Honolulu, HI 96817-2704
Phone: (808) 847-3511
Internet: http://www.bishop.hawaii.org/bishop/library/library.html

Open 9 a.m. to 5 p.m. every day except December 25th

East-West Center Research Information Services
John A. Burns Hall
1601 East-West Rd.
Honolulu, HI 96848-1601
Fax: (808) 944-7670
Reference Room (Room 4063): (808) 944-7345
Periodicals Room (Room 4066): (808) 944-7451
Internet: http://www.ewc.hawaii.edu/ris/ris1.htm
Research Information Specialist: Phyllis Tabusa

- open Monday through Friday from 8 a.m. to 4:30 p.m., except for federal holidays.
- library collection houses approximately 27,000 books, 17,000 unpublished documents and reprints, 1000 periodical titles, CD-ROM and diskette publications and vertical files on subjects, countries and agencies relevant to Center activities

- *Collection features a current and interdisciplinary coverage of social, cultural, political and economic development issues in Asia and the Pacific region.*

Hamilton Library – Hawaiian Collection
Center for Hawaiian Studies
University of Hawaii at Manoa
(see *Special Centers* for address)

The world's foremost collection of 19th and 20th century published materials about the Hawaiian Islands.

Maui Historical Society and Bailey House Museum
2375-A Main St.
Wailuku, HI 96793
Phone: (808) 244-3326
Fax: (808) 244-3920

Dedicated to the preservation and understanding of Maui's history, the museum collects and holds materials and information related to history of Maui.

Popular Media

Film and Video Center
National Museum of the American Indian
George Gustav Heye Center
Phone: (212) 514-3737
E-mail: fvc@ic.si.edu

Dedicated to public programs and information services concerning film, video, radio, and electronic media by and about indigenous peoples of North, Central, and South America and Hawaii. Media collection houses 1500 titles. A selection of 250 videotapes is available for viewing without appointment in the museum's Resource Center. Museum does not sell or lend films and video.

Colleges/Universities

Chaminade University of Honolulu

3140 Waialae Ave.

Honolulu, HI 96816-1587

Phone: (808) 735-4711

Fax: (808) 739-4647

Internet: http://www.chaminade.edu

President: Sue Wessel Kamper

- private, 4-year liberal arts university affiliated with the Roman Catholic Marianists.
- library collection houses approximately 70,000 books, serial backfiles and government documents, 822 current serials, 28 microforms and an audio/visual viewing room.

Denver Business College

419 South Street, Suite 174

Honolulu, HI 96813

Phone: (808) 942-1000

Fax: (808) 533-3064

Internet: http://www.dbc.edu

Director: Jerry Warren

- private, 2-year college
- library collection houses approximately 3000 books, serial backfiles and government documents, 50 current serials, and 50 audio and visual materials.

Hawaii Business College

33 South King St., 4th Floor

Honolulu, HI 96813-4316

Phone: (808) 524-4014

Fax: (808) 524-0284

President: Mitsuru Omori

- private, vocational college
- quarter system

Hawaii Community College

200 W. Kawili St.

Hilo, HI 96720-4091

Phone: (808) 974-7662

Fax: (808) 974-7692

Internet: http://www.hawcc.hawaii.edu

Provost: Sandra Sakaguchi

Public, 2-year liberal arts college.

Heald Business College

1500 Kapiolani Rd.

Honolulu, HI 96814

Phone: (808) 955-1500

Internet: http://www.heald.edu

Director: Evelyn Schemmel

Private, 2-year college.

Honolulu Community College

874 Dillingham Blvd.

Honolulu, HI 96817

Phone: (808) 845-9211

Fax: (808) 845-9173

Internet: http://www.hcc.hawaii.edu

Provost: Peter Kessinger

- public, 2-year college
- library collection houses approximately 54,356 books, serial backfiles and government documents, 243 current serials (including periodicals and newspapers) and 66,510 microforms

Kapiolani Community College

4303 Diamond Head Rd.

Honolulu, HI 96816

Phone: (808) 734-9111

Internet: http://naio.kcc.hawaii.edu

Provost: John Morton

Public, 2-year college.

Kauai Community College

3-1901 Kaumualii Hwy.

Lihue, HI 96766

Phone: (808) 245-8311

Fax: (808) 245-8220

Internet: http://www.kauaicc.hawaii.edu

Provost: David Iha

- public, 2-year college
- library collection houses approximately 47,848 books, serial backfiles and government documents, 277 current serials, 286 microforms and 2331 audio and visual materials

Leeward Community College

96-045 Ala Ike

Pearl City, HI 96782

Phone: (808) 455-0011

Internet: http://lccada.lcc.hawaii.edu

Provost: Barbara Polk

Public, 2-year liberal arts college.

Maui Community College

310 Kaahumanu Ave.

Kahului, HI 96732

Phone: (808) 984-3500

Fax: (808) 242-9618

Internet: http://mccinfo.mauicc.hawaii.edu/menu.html

Provost: Clyde Sakamoto

Public, 2-year liberal arts college.

University of Hawaii at Hilo

200 W. Kawili St.

Hilo, HI 96720-4091

Phone: (808) 974-7311

Fax: (808) 974-7622

Internet: http://www2.hawaii.edu/~uhhilo

Chancellor: William A. Pearman

- public, 4-year liberal arts university
- library collection houses approximately 240,000 books, serial backfiles and government documents, 351,200 current serials and contains Hawaiian special collections

University of Hawaii at Manoa
2444 Dole St.
Honolulu, HI 96822
Phone: (808) 956-8111
Internet: http://www.hawaii.edu
Provost: Kenneth P. Mortimer

- public, 4-year liberal arts university
- library collection houses approximately 1,959,713 books, serial backfiles and government documents, 26,900 current serials, 18,858 microforms, 35,111 audio and visual materials and contains Asian, Hawaiian and Pacific collections

University of Hawaii, West Oahu
96-043 Ala Ike St.
Pearl City, HI 96782
Phone: (808) 453-6565
Fax: (808) 453-6075
Internet: http://www.uhwo.hawaii.edu
Chancellor: Kenneth Perrin

- public, upper-division liberal arts university
- library collection houses approximately 25,000 books, serial backfiles and government documents, 135 serials and 5500 microforms

Windward Community College

45-720 Keaahala Rd.

Kaneohe, HI 96744

Phone: (808) 235-0077

Internet: http://www.wcc.hawaii.edu

Provost: Peter Dyer

Public, 2-year college.

Special Programs

Hawaiian Studies Department
University of Hawaii at Hilo

(see *Colleges/Universities* for address)

Phone: (808) 974-7339

Fax: (808) 974-7737

Internet: http://www.uhh.hawaii.edu

E-mail: shhadm@hawaii.edu

- offers a major and minor in Hawaiian Studies
- certificate in Hawaiian Language and culture

Special Centers

Center for Hawaiian Studies
University of Hawaii at Manoa

Hawaiian Studies Bldg., Room 209A

2645 Dole St.

Honolulu, HI 96822

Phone: (808) 973-0989

Fax: (808) 973-0988

E-mail: chsuhm@hawaii.edu

Director: Lilikala Kame'eleihiwa

Through student services, instruction, research and community outreach, the Center dedicates itself to serving the Native people of Hawaii from Ni'ihau to Hawaii Island..

Hale Kuamo'o Hawaiian Language Center

University of Hawaii at Hilo

Room 215, Edith Kanaka'ole Hall

Hilo, HI 96720-4091

Phone: (808) 933-3339

Internet: http://www.olelo.hawaii.edu/op/orgs/uhhmh/

Contact: Kalena Silva

Publishers

Hawaii Hochi, Ltd.

917 Kokea St.

Honolulu, HI U.S.A.

Phone: (808) 845-2255

Fax: (808) 847-7215

President: Paul Yempuku

Internet: http://www.sbs-np.co.jp/hawaii/index.html

Hawaii Hochi publishes The Hawaii Hochi, which is the only Japanese daily newspaper in Hawaii, English Journal, The Hawaii Herald, Aloha Paradise

Guide, which is familiar to Japanese tourists. They also publish *Island Trends,* a monthly newspaper, and *Aloha Annual, which is an almanac in Japanese about Hawaii.*

IV. Hispanic-Americans

Libraries and Archival Resources

Arizona Collection – Chicano Studies Library Project
Arizona State University
Hayden Library
Tempe, AZ 85281

Library of Congress – Hispanic Division
Thomas Jefferson Building, Room 239E
Washington, DC 20540

National Association Pro Spanish Speaking Elderly - Library
3875 Wilshire Blvd., Suite 401
Los Angeles, CA 90010

Oakland Public Library – Latin American Library
1900 Fruitvale Ave., Suite 1-A
Oakland, CA 94601

The Penny Lernoux Memorial Library on Latin America
Resource Center of the Americas
317 17th Ave. SE
Minneapolis, MN 55414-2077
Phone: (612) 627-9445
Fax: (612) 627-9450
Internet: http://www.americas.org
E-mail: info@americas.org

A unique collection of 7000 books, 150 periodicals, and 250 videos in Spanish and English, the library is open free of charge for study, research and browsing, from 11am-7pm, Monday-Thursday, and 11am-4pm, Friday.

Reference Library
University Boricua
Puerto Rican Research and Resources Center, Inc.
1766 Church St.
Washington, DC 20036

University of Puerto Rico – Puerto Rican Collection
Box CUPR Station
Rio Piedras, PR 00931

Popular Media

El Andar Magazine
PO Box 7745
Santa Cruz, CA 95060
Phone: (831) 457-8353
Fax: (831) 457-8354
Internet: http://www.mercado.com/andar/info.html
E-mail: info@elandar.com

National magazine devoted to discussion of contemporary Latino cultures in the Americas.

Frontera Magazine
PO Box 30529
Los Angeles, CA 90030

Phone: (213) 975-9411

Internet: http://www.fronteramag.com/

E-mail: frontmag@aol.com

Magazine devoted to *Latino music, art and culture for a new generation..*

Hispanic Times Magazine

PO Box 579

Winchester, CA 92596

Internet: http://www.hispanictimesmag.com

Diverse magazine directed toward college-educated Latinos.

Latina Magazine

1500 Broadway, Suite 600

New York, NY 10036

Internet: http://www.latina.com

Slick new magazine devoted to topics of interest to young Latinas.

Latina Style Magazine

Internet: http://www.latinastyle.com

The only 100% Latina-owned national publication in the U.S. Content is directed toward professional-minded Latinas.

Latino USA: The Radio Journal of News and Culture

Internet: http://www.latinousa.org/index.html

Website for the nationwide program.

"Sin Fronteras" (Without Borders)

PO Box 190922

Dallas, TX 75219-0922

Phone: (214) 826-8869

Fax: (214) 821-4048

E-mail: SinFronteras@worldnet.att.net

A bilingual radio program, broadcast on KNON (89.3FM) from 10pm to midnight, with music (English, Spanish, World Beat), news, commentary and interviews with artists, civic leaders, and politicians. Also represents the Gay and Lesbian Latino community.

Urban Latino

Internet: http://www.urbanlatino.com/magazine/main.html

Written by and for Latinos, this online magazine examines the Latino experience in the United States from a variety of perspectives.

Colleges/Universities

(from the Office of Civil Rights, U.S. Dept. of Education)

Adams State College

208 Edgemont Blvd.

Alamosa, CO 81102

President: W.M. Fulkerson, Jr.

American University of Puerto Rico

PO Box 708

Manati, PR 00701

Arizona Western College
PO Box 929
Yuma, AZ 85366
President: James Carruthers

Atlantic College
PO Box 1774
Guaynabo, PR 00970
President: Teresa De Dios-Unanue

Bakersfield College
1801 Panorama Dr.
Bakersfield, CA 93305-1299
President: Richard Wright

Bayamon Central University
PO Box 1725
Bayamon, PR 00960-1725
President: Father Van Rooij

Bee County College
3800 Charco Rd.
Beeville, TX 78102
President: Norman Wallace

Berkeley
44 Riffle Camp Rd.
West Paterson, NJ 07424

Berkeley College of New York
3 E. 43rd St.

New York, NY 10017
President: Glen Zeitzer

California State University - Dominguez Hills

1000 E. Victoria St.
Carson, CA 90747
President: Robert C. Detweiler

California State University - Los Angeles

5151 State University Dr.
Los Angeles, CA 90032
President: James M. Rosser

Caribbean Center for Advanced Studies

Box 3711 Old San Juan Station
San Juan, PR 00902-3711
President: Salvador Santiago-Negron

Caribbean University – Bayamon

CARR 167 KM 21.2
Bayamon, PR 00960-0493
President: Angel Juan Ortega

Caribbean University – Carolina

Apartado 4760
Carolina, PR 00984
President: Angel Juan Ortega

Caribbean University – Ponce

Box 7733
Castillo & Mayer Street

Ponce, PR 00731

President: Angel Juan Ortega

Caribbean University – Vega Baja

Box 4258, Carretera 671

Vega Baja, PR 00694

President: Angel Juan Ortega

Center for Advanced Studies on Puerto Rico & The Caribbean

PO Box S4467

Old San Juan, PR 00904

Executive Director: Ricardo E. Alegria

Center for Northern Studies

RFD Box 1860

Wolcott, VT 05680

Central Arizona College

8470 N. Overfield Rd.

Coolidge, AZ 85228-9778

President: John J. Klein

Cerritos College

11110 Alondra Blvd.

Norwalk, CA 90650

Interim Superintendent: Fred Gaskin

Chaffey Community College

5885 Haven Ave.

Rancho Cucamonga, CA 91737-3002

Superintendent/President: Jerry Young

Citrus College
1000 W. Foothill Blvd.
Glendora, CA 91741-1899

Cochise College
4190 W. Hwy. 80
Douglas, AZ 85607-9724
President: Dr. Walter Patton

Colegio Biblico Pentecostal De Puerto Rico
Box 901
Saint Just, PR 00750
President: Rev. Ismael Lopez Borrero

Colegio Tecnologico Del Municipio De San Juan
Jose Oliver St., Tres Monjitas
Hato Rey, PR 00918
Chancellor: Peter J.L. De Menkini

Colegio Universitario Bautista De Puerto Rico
PO Box 403
Bayamon, PR 00960

Colegio Universitario Del Este
PO Box 2010
Carolina, PR 00983-2010
Chancellor: Alberto Maldonado

College of Aeronautics
La Guardia Airport

Flushing, NY 11371
President: Richard B. Goetze, Jr.

College of The Sequoias
915 S. Mooney Blvd.
Visalia, CA 93277
Acting President/Superintendent: David Erickson

College of The Southwest – Carlsbad
408 W. McKay
Carlsbad, NM 88220
President: Joan M. Tucker

Columbia College
CARR 183 KM 17
Caguas, PR 00726
Branch Director: Carmen M. Rivera

Community College of Denver
PO Box 173363
Denver, CO 80217
President: Byron McClenney

Conservatory of Music of Puerto Rico
Box 41227 Minillas Station
Santurce, PR 00940-1227
Chancellor: Dr. Raymond Torres-Santos

CUNY Borough of Manhattan Community College
199 Chambers St.
New York, NY 10007

Acting President: Marcia V. Keizs

CUNY Bronx Community College
W. 181st St. & University Ave.

Bronx, NY 10453

Acting President: Leo A. Corbie

CUNY City College
Convent Ave. at 138th St.

New York, NY 10031

President: Yolanda T. Moses

CUNY Hostos Community College
500 Grand Concourse

Bronx, NY 10451

President: Isaura Santiago-Santiago

CUNY John Jay College of Criminal Justice
899 10th Ave.

New York, NY 10019

President: Gerald W. Lynch

CUNY La Guardia Community College
31-10 Thomson Ave.

Long Island City, NY 11101

President: Raymond C. Bowen

CUNY Lehman College
Bedford Park Blvd., W.

Bronx, NY 10468

President: Ricardo R. Fernandez

Del Mar College
101 Baldwin
Corpus Christi, TX 78404-3897
President: B.R. Venters

DeVry Institute of Technology - Pomona
901 Corporate
Pomona, CA 91768
President: David G. Moore

Don Bosco Technical Institute
1151 San Gabriel Blvd.
Rosemead, CA 91770-4299
President: Nicholas Reina

East Los Angeles College
1301 Brooklyn Ave.
Monterey Park, CA 91754
President: Ernest Moreno

Eastern New Mexico University – Roswell Campus
PO Box 6000
52 University Blvd.
Roswell, NM 88202
President: Loyd R. Hughes

Electronic Data Processing College of PR Inc.
Muñoz Rivera 555
Hato Rey, PR 00918
President: Anibel Nieves

Escuela De Artes Plasticas – ICPR
PO Box 4184
San Juan, PR 00905
Chancellor: Marimar Benitez

Fashion Institute of Design and Merchandising - San Diego
San Diego, CA 92101
President: Tonian Hohberg

Florida International University
University Park
Miami, FL 33199
President: Modesto Maidique

Fresno City College
1101 E. University Ave.
Fresno, CA 93741
President: Dr. Brice Harris

Gavilan College
5055 Santa Teresa Blvd.
Gilroy, CA 95020
Superintendent/President: Dr. Glenn E. Mayle

Hartnell College
156 Homestead Ave.
Salinas, CA 93901
Superintendent/President: Leonard A. Grandy

Heritage College

3240 Fort Rd.

Toppenish, WA 98948

President: Kathleen Ross

Houston Community College System

22 Waugh Dr.

PO Box 7849

Houston, TX 77270-7849

Hudson County Community College

901 Bergen Ave.

Jersey City, NJ 07306

President: Glen Gabert

Huertas Junior College

Box 8429, Hector R. Bunker 41 S

Caguas, PR 00726

President: F. Rodriquez Matos

Humacao Community College

101-103 Cruz Ortiz Stella Ave.

Humacao, PR 00792

ICPR Junior College – Arecibo

CARR 2 KM 80 4 BO San Daniel

Arecibo, PR 00614-0067

ICPR Junior College – General Institutional

558 Muñoz Rivera Ave.

Hato Rey, PR 00919-0304

Chancellor: Genoveva Christian

ICPR Junior College – Mayaguez
McKinley 80 Oeste
Mayaguez, PR 00681-1108
Dean Director: Genoveva Christian

Imperial Valley College
PO Box 158
Imperial, CA 92251-0158
Superintendent/President: John Depaoli

Incarnate Word College
4301 Broadway
San Antonio, TX 78209
President: Louis J. Agnese, Jr.

Indiana College of Commerce
7147 Kennedy Ave.
Hammond, IN 46323

Instituto De Educación Universal – Rio Piedras
Apartado 3818 San Jose Contrac
Rio Piedras, PR 00930

Instituto De Educación Universal – Sabana Seca
PO Box 1027
Sabana Seca, PR 00749

Inter American University of Puerto Rico – Aguadilla
Comercio 21, PO Box 925
Aguadilla, PR 00605

Chancellor: Hilda Baco

Inter American University of Puerto Rico – Arecibo
BO San Daniel, PO Box 845
Arecibo, PR 00613
Chancellor: Zalda Vega

Inter American University of Puerto Rico – Barranquitas
PO Box 517
Barranquitas, PR 00794
Chancellor: Vidal Rivera

Inter American University of Puerto Rico – Bayamon
Carretera 174, Urb. Industrial M
Bayamon, PR 00620
Chancellor: Felix Torres Leon

Inter American University of Puerto Rico – Fajardo
PO Box 1029
Fajardo, PR 00738
Chancellor: Yolanda Robles

Inter American University of Puerto Rico – Guayama
Call Box 10004
Guayama, PR 00785
Chancellor: Samuel F. Febres Santiago

Inter American University of Puerto Rico – Metro
Box 1293
Hato Rey, PR 00919
Chancellor: Manuel J. Fernos

Inter American University of Puerto Rico – Ponce

Barrio Sabanetas Carretera 1

Ponce, PR 00731

Chancellor: Marilina Wayland

Inter American University of Puerto Rico – San German

Call Box 5100

San German, PR 00753

Chancellor: Agnes Mojica

Inter American University of Puerto Rico – School of Law

Box 70351

San Juan, PR 00936-8351

Dean: C. Ramos Gonzalez

Inter American University of Puerto Rico – School of Optometry

Box 191049

Hato Rey, PR 00919-1049

Dean: Arthur J. Afanador

ITT Technical Institute – Albuquerque

5100 Masthead NE

Albuquerque, NM 87109

Director: Marianne Rittner

ITT Technical Institute – Houston

9421 W. Sam Houston Pkwy.

Houston, TX 77099

Center Director: D. Louis Christensen

ITT Technical Institute - San Diego

9680 Granite Ridge Dr.

San Diego, CA 92123

Director: Robert Hammond

ITT Technical Institute - Tucson

1840 E. Benson Hwy.

Tucson, AZ 85714

Director: William C. Fennelly

ITT Technical Institute - West Covina (CA)

1530 W. Cameron Ave.

West Covina, CA 91790

Director: Michele Huggard

Jones College – Miami Campus

5975 Sunset Dr.

Miami, FL 33143

Vice President/Director: Nancy Rodriguez

Kings River Community College

995 N. Reed

Reedley, CA 93654

President: Richard J. Giese

Laredo Community College

West End Washington St.

Laredo, TX 78040

President: Roger Worsley

Los Angeles Harbor College

1111 Figueroa Pl.

Wilmington, CA 90744

President: James Heinselman

Los Angeles Trade Technical College

400 W. Washington Blvd.

Los Angeles, CA 90015-4181

President: Thomas L. Stevens, Jr.

Los Angeles City College

855 N. Vermont Ave.

Los Angeles, CA 90029

President: Jose Robledo

Los Angeles Mission College

1310 San Fernando Rd.

San Fernando, CA 91340

President: Dr. Jack Fujimoto

MacCormac College

506 S. Wabash

Chicago, IL 60605

President: John H. Allen

Medical Center of Delaware - School for EMT Training

PO Box 1668

Wilmington, DE 19899

Merced College

3600 M St.

Merced, CA 95348-2898

Superintendent/President: E. Jan Moser

Miami-Dade Community College
300 NE 2nd Ave.
Miami, FL 33132
President: Robert McCabe

Monroe College – Main Campus
Monroe College Way
Bronx, NY 10468
President: Stephen J. Jerome

Mount Saint Mary's College
12001 Chalon Rd.
Los Angeles, CA 90049
President: Karen Kennelly

MT San Antonio College
1100 N. Grand
Walnut, CA 91789
President/Superintendent: William Feddersen

National College of Business & Technology – Arecibo
109 Gonzalo Marin St.
Arecibo, PR 00612
Executive Director: Iride M. Dumantt

National College of Business & Technology – Bayamon
ST RD 2 Ramos Bldg.
Bayamon, PR 00960
President: Jesus Siverio

The National Hispanic University
135 Gish Rd.
San Jose, CA 95112

Newark School of Fine and Industrial Arts
550 Dr. Martin Luther King, Jr. Blvd.
Newark, NJ 07102

New Mexico Highlands University
University Ave.
Las Vegas, NM 87701
President: Gilbert Sanchez

New Mexico State University – Carlsbad
1500 University Dr.
Carlsbad, NM 88220
Provost: Douglas Burgham

New Mexico State University – Dona Ana
Box 30001, Dept. 3DA
Las Cruces, NM 88003-0105
Campus Director: James L. McLaughlin

New Mexico State University – Grants
1500 3rd St.
Grants, NM 87020
Campus Director: David Leas

New Mexico State University – Main Campus
Box 30001, Dept. 3Z

Las Cruces, NM 88003

Interim President: William Conroy

Northern New Mexico Community College

1002 N. Onate St.

Española, NM 87532

President: Connie A. Valdez

Oblate School of Theology

285 Oblate Dr.

San Antonio, TX 78216-6693

President: Patrick Guidon

Odessa College

201 W. University

Odessa, TX 79764

President: Philip Speegle

Otero Junior College

1802 Colorado Ave.

La Junta, CO 81050

President: J. Treece

Our Lady of The Lake University – San Antonio

411 SW 24th St.

San Antonio, TX 78207-4689

President: Elizabeth Sueltenfuss

Oxnard College

4000 S. Rose Ave.

Oxnard, CA 93033

128

President: Elise Schneider

Palo Alto College

1400 Villaret

San Antonio, TX 78224

Interim President: Dr. Joel Vela

Palo Verde College

811 W. Chanslor Way

Blythe, CA 92225

Superintendent/President: Wilford J. Beumel

Parks College

1023 Tijeras NW

Albuquerque, NM 87102

President: Cynthia Welch

Passaic County Community College

College Blvd.

Paterson, NJ 07509

President: Elliot Collins

Phillips College - Inland Empire Campus

4300 Central Ave.

Riverside, CA 92506

President: Angela Hughes

Phillips Junior College

2048 N. Fine Ave.

Fresno, CA 93727

Director: Richard Melella

Phillips Junior College
8520 Balboa Blvd.
Northridge, CA 91325
Director: Tom Azim-Zadeh

Plaza Business Institute
74-9 37th Ave.
Jackson Heights, NY 11372
President: Charles Callahan

Ponce School of Medicine
PO Box 7004, University St.
Ponce, PR 00732
President/Dean: Jaime Rivera Dueño

Pontifical Catholic University of Puerto Rico – Guayama
PO Box 809
Guayama, PR 00784
Dean Director: A. Sanchez Otero

Pontifical Catholic University of Puerto Rico – Mayaguez
Centro De Mayaguez, PO Box 1326
Mayaguez, PR 00681-1326
Dean-Director: Jaime Ortiz Vega

Pontifical Catholic University of Puerto Rico – Ponce
2250 Ave. Las Americas
Ponce, PR 00731
President: Tosello Giangiacomo

Porterville College

100 E. College Ave.

Porterville, CA 93257

President: Dr. Bonnie L. Rogers

Pueblo Community College

900 W. Orman Ave.

Pueblo, CO 81004

President: Joe D. May

Ramirez College of Business & Technology

103 Muñoz Rivera Ave.

PO Box 8074

Hato Rey, PR 00918

President: Rogena Kyles

Rancho Santiago College

17th at Bristol

Santa Ana, CA 92706

Chancellor: Vivian Blevins

Rhode Island Hospital - School of Ultra Sonography

593 Eddy St.

Providence, RI 02903

Rio Hondo College

3600 Workman Mill Rd.

Whittier, CA 90601-1699

Interim Superintendent/President: Timothy M. Wood

Robert Morris College

180 N. La Salle St.

Chicago, IL 60601

President: Richard Pickett

Saint Augustine College

1333 W. Argyle

Chicago, IL 60640

President: Carlos Plazas

Saint Edward's University

3001 S. Congress Ave.

Austin, TX 78704-6489

President: Patricia Hayes

Saint John Vianney College Seminary

2900 SW 87th Ave.

Miami, FL 33165

President/Rector: George Garcia

Saint Mary's University

One Camino Santa Maria

San Antonio, TX 78228-8572

President: John Moder

Saint Phillip's College

1801 Martin Luther King Dr.

San Antonio, TX 78203

Interim President: Byron Skinner

Saint Thomas University

16400 NW 32nd Ave.

Miami, FL 33054

President: Monsignor Franklyn M. Casale

San Antonio College

1300 San Pedro Ave.

San Antonio, TX 78284

President: Ruth Burgos Sasscer

San Antonio Training Division

9350 S. Presa

San Antonio, TX 78223-4799

San Bernardino Valley College

701 S. Mount Vernon Ave.

San Bernardino, CA 92410-2798

Chancellor: Stuart M. Bundy

Santa Fe Community College

South Richards Ave., PO Box 4187

Santa Fe, NM 87502-4187

President: Leonardo De La Garza

Sawyer College at Ventura

2101 E. Gonzales Rd.

Oxnard, CA 93030

President: Doreen Adamache

South Mountain Community College

7050 S. 24th St.

Phoenix, AZ 85040

President: John D. Cordova

South Plains College

1401 College Ave.

Levelland, TX 79336

President: Gary McDaniel

Southwest College Institute for The Deaf

Ave. C

Big Spring, TX 79720

Southwestern College

900 Otay Lakes Rd.

Chula Vista, CA 92010

Superintendent/President: Joseph M. Conte

Southwest Institute of Merchandising and Design

9611 Acer Ave.

El Paso, TX 79925

Vice President: Jesse L. Simon

Southwest Texas Junior College

2401 Garner Field Rd.

Uvalde, TX 78801

Spertus College

618 S. Michigan Ave.

Chicago, IL 60605

President: Howard Sulkin

Sul Ross State University

Alpine, TX 79832

President: Vic Morgan

Technical Career Institutes
320 W. 31st St.
New York, NY 10001
President: Eric Biederman

Texas A&I University
Santa Gertrudis
Kingsville, TX 78363

Texas A&M International University
West End Washington St.
Laredo, TX 78040

Texas A&M University – Corpus Christi
6300 Ocean Dr.
Corpus Christi, TX 78412
President: Robert R. Furgason

Texas A&M University – Kingsville
Santa Gertrudis
Kingsville, TX 78363
President: Manuel L. Ibanez

Texas Southmost College
80 Fort Brown
Brownsville, TX 78520
Executive Director: Michael Putegnat

Texas State Technical College – Harlingen Campus

2424 Boxwood

Harlingen, TX 78550-3697

Campus President: J. Gilbert Leal

Trinidad State Junior College

600 Prospect St.

Trinidad, CO 81082

President: Harold Deseums

Trinity College at Miami

500 NE 1st Ave.

PO Box 019674

Miami, FL 33101-9674

President: Kenneth M. Meyer

Universidad Adventista De Las Antillas

Box 118

Mayaguez, PR 00681

President: Miguel Muñoz

Universidad Central Del Caribe

Ramon Ruiz Arnau University Ho.

Laurel Ave.

Bayamon, PR 00960

President: Raul Marcial Rojas

Universidad Del Turabo

PO Box 3030, University Station

Turabo, PR 00778

Chancellor: Dennis Alicea

Universidad Metropolitana

Call Box 21150

Rio Piedras, PR 00928

Chancellor: Rene La Barca

Universidad Politecnica De Puerto Rico

Avenida Ponce De Leon, Suite 405

San Juan, PR 00918

President: Ernesto V. Barquet

University of Houston – Downtown

1 Main St., Suite 919S

Houston, TX 77002

President: Max Castillo

University of New Mexico – Los Alamos

4000 University Dr.

Los Alamos, NM 87544

Director: Dr. Carlos Ramirez

University of New Mexico – Main Campus

Albuquerque, NM 87131

President: Richard Teck

University of New Mexico – Valencia Campus

280 La Entrada

Los Lunas, NM 87031

Interim Director: Phyllis A. Mingus-Pepin

University of Phoenix – Puerto Rico Campus

PO Box 3870

Guaynabo, PR 00970-3870
Rector: Candida R.T. Acosta

University of Puerto Rico – Aguadilla Regional College
Box 160
Ramey, PR 00604
Acting Director: Nelson Hereadi Borges

University of Puerto Rico – Arecibo Campus
Finca Las Dunas Carretera 653 Ruta
Arecibo, PR 00613
Dean-Director: Juan Ramirez Silva

University of Puerto Rico – Bayamon Tech. University College
Carretera 174 Minillas
Bayamon, PR 00959-1919
Dean-Director: Carmen A. Rivera

University of Puerto Rico – Carolina Regional College
PO Box 4800
Carolina, PR 00984-4800
Dean-Director: Luz Lafontaine

University of Puerto Rico - Cayey University College
Antonio R. Barcelo Ave.
Cayey, PR 00633
Chancellor: Jose L. Monserrate

University of Puerto Rico – Humacao University College
CUH Station
Humacao, PR 00791

Chancellor: Dr. Roberto Marrero

University of Puerto Rico – La Montana Regional College
PO Box 2500
Utuado, PR 00641
Dean-Director: Ramon A. Toro

University of Puerto Rico – Mayaguez
Post St.
Mayaguez, PR 00681
Chancellor: Dr. Stuart J. Ramos Biaggi

University of Puerto Rico – Medical Sciences Campus
PO Box 365067
San Juan, PR 00936
Chancellor: Dr. Jorge L. Sanchez

University of Puerto Rico – Ponce Technical University College
PO Box 7186
Ponce, PR 00732
Acting Dean & Director: Ruth Calzada

University of Sacred Heart
PO Box 12383, Loiza Station
Santurce, PR 00914
President: Jose Jaime Rivera

University of Saint Thomas
3800 Montrose Blvd.
Houston, TX 77006
President: Joseph M. McFadden

The University of Texas at Brownsville
80 Fort Brown
Brownsville, TX 78520-4991
President: Juliet Garcia

The University of Texas at El Paso
500 W. University Ave.
El Paso, TX 79968
President: Diana Natalicio

The University of Texas – Pan American at Edinburg
1201 W. University Dr.
Edinburg, TX 78539
President: Miguel Nevarez

The University of Texas at San Antonio
6900 N. Loop 1604 W.
San Antonio, TX 78249-0616
President: Samuel Kirkpatrick

University of The Virgin Islands
2 John Brewer's Bay
Charlotte Amalie, VI 00802-9990
President: Orville Kean

University of The Virgin Islands – Kingshill
RR 02 Box 10000
Kingshill, VI 00850
President: Orville Kean

Utah Valley Hospital - School of Radiologic Technology

1034 N. 5th W. St.

Provo, UT 84603

Valley Baptist Medical Center – School of Vocational Nursing

PO Drawer 2588

Harlingen, TX 78550

Ventura College

4667 Telegraph Rd.

Ventura, CA 93003

President: Jesus Carreon

Veterans Affairs Medical Center - School of Med. Tech.

5901 E. 7th St., Suite 113ED

Long Beach, CA 90822

Western New Mexico University

1000 College Ave.

Silver City, NM 88061

President: Dr. John Counts

West Hills Community College

300 Cherry Ln.

Coalinga, CA 93210

President/Superintendent: Dr. Frank G. Gornick

Whittier College

13406 E. Philadelphia St.

Whittier, CA 90601

President: James L. Ash, Jr.

Wiley College
711 Wiley Ave.
Marshall, TX 75670
President: Lamore J. Carter

Woodbury University
7500 Glen Oaks Blvd.
Burbank, CA 91510-7846
President: Paul E. Sago

Wood Tobe-Coburn School
8 E. 40th St.
New York, NY 10016
President: Rosemary Duggan

Special Programs

Latin American Studies
Center for Interdisciplinary Studies
Loyola University, Chicago
Lake Shore Campus, Damen Hall 105
6525 N. Sheridan Rd.
Chicago, IL 60626
Phone: (773) 508-2935
Fax: (773) 508-8797
Internet: http://www.luc.edu/depts/latin_am_st

Offers an interdisciplinary minor.

Latin American Studies Program
Jackson School of International Studies
University of Washington
Box 353650
Seattle, WA 98195-3650
Phone: (206) 543-4370
Fax: (206) 616-3170
E-mail: jsisinfo@u.washington.edu

Offers a BA in International Studies with a concentration in Latin American Studies. *Graduate students may also work towards a Bachelor of Arts degree in Latin American Studies while pursuing graduate degrees in other departments.*

Special Centers

Spanish Colonial Research Center
Zimmerman Library – University of New Mexico
Albuquerque, NM 87131
Phone: (505) 766-8743
Director: Dr. Joseph P. Sánchez
Internet: http://www.unm.edu/~clahr/scrc.html

Contains collection of microfilms, maps, architectural plans and sketches from Spanish and Mexican archives for those interested in colonial Latin American history.

Publishers

Curbstone Press

321 Jackson St.

Willimantic, CT 06226

Phone: (860) 423-5110

Fax: (860) 423-9242

Internet: curbstone@connix.com

Independent press since 1945, specializing in Latin-American literature.

Exodus

Internet: www.exodusltd.com

Fundacion Historica Tavera

HISPANIC Publishing Corporation

98 San Jacinto Blvd., Suite 1150

Austin, TX 78701-4039

Phone: (512) 476-5599

Fax: (512) 320-1942

Publishes HISPANIC magazine, Moderna: the Latina Magazine, and HISPANIC Online, found on America Online and the WWW. Based in Austin, TX, a 100% minority-owned company controlled by the Estrada family.

The Latin American Bookstore, Ltd.

204 N. Geneva St.

Ithaca, NY 14850

Phone: (607) 273-2418

Fax: (607) 273-6003

Internet: libros@latinamericanbooks.com

Since 1982, a distributor of Latin American and Spanish publications to surrounding libraries.

Government Programs

Agency for International Development

Ronald Reagan Building

Washington, DC 20523-1000

Phone: (202) 712-4810

Fax: (202) 216-3524

Internet: http://www.info.usaid.gov

Federal agency that effects international aid programs in order *to advance the political and economic interests of the United States.*

Commission on Civil Rights

624 9th Street, NW

Washington, D.C. 20425

Western Regional Office

Suite 810

3660 Wilshire Boulevard

Los Angeles, California 90010

Contact: Philip Montez, Director

Phone: (213) 894-3437

Internet: http://www.usccr.gov

The U.S. Commission on Civil Rights is an independent, bipartisan agency first established by Congress in 1957 and reestablished in 1983. It is directed to:

- *Investigate complaints alleging that citizens are being deprived of their right to vote by reason of their race, color, religion, sex, age, disability, or national origin, or by reason of fraudulent practices;*
- *Study and collect information relating to discrimination or a denial of equal protection of the laws under the Constitution because of race, color, religion, sex, age, disability, or national origin, or in the administration of justice;*
- *Appraise Federal laws and policies with respect to discrimination or denial of equal protection of the laws because of race, color, religion, sex, age, disability, or national origin, or in the administration of justice;*
- *Serve as a national clearinghouse for information in respect to discrimination or denial of equal protection of the laws because of race, color, religion, sex, age, disability, or national origin;*
- *Submit reports, findings, and recommendations to the President and Congress;*
- *Issue public service announcements to discourage discrimination or denial of equal protection of the laws.*

Department of Commerce
Census Bureau
American Fact Finder

Internet: http://factfinder.census.gov/java_prod/dads.ui.homePage.HomePage

Provides information from 1990 census in a variety of forms. Allows the user to create profiles of almost any American community or region based on demographics data such as income and more.

Minority Business Development Agency
14th St. & Constitution Ave., NW

Room 5055

Washington, DC 20230

Internet: http://www.mbda.gov

Feedback Form: http://www.mbda.gov/contact.asp

The Minority Business Development Agency (MBDA), is part of the U.S. Department of Commerce. MBDA is the only Federal Agency created specifically to foster the creation, growth and expansion of minority-owned businesses in America.

Department of Education
Office of Bilingual Education and Minority Languages Affairs

600 Independence Avenue, SW

Washington, DC 20202-6510

Internet: http://www.ed.gov/offices/OBEMLA

E-mail: askncbe@ncbe.gwu.edu

Contact: Art Love, Acting Director

Phone: (202) 205-5463

E-mail: art_love@ed.gov

Congress passed the Bilingual Education Act in 1968 in recognition of the growing number of linguistically and culturally diverse children enrolled in schools who, because of their limited English proficiency, were not receiving an education equal to their English-proficient peers. The purpose of this Act was, and continues to be, aligned with Title VI of the Civil Rights Act of 1964 which the Department interprets as follows:

Where inability to speak and understand the English language excludes national origin minority group children from effective participation in the educational program offered by a school district, the district must take affirmative steps to rectify the language deficiency in order to open its instructional program to these students.

Established in 1974 by Congress, the Office of Bilingual Education and Minority Languages Affairs helps school districts meet their responsibility to provide equal education opportunity to limited English proficient children.

Office for Civil Rights

Customer Service Team

Mary E. Switzer Building

330 C Street, SW

Washington, DC 20202

Phone: (202) 205-5413; 1-800-421-3481

Fax: (202) 205-9862

Internet: http://www.ed.gov/offices/OCR

E-mail: OCR@ED.Gov

Assistant Secretary Office of Civil Rights: Norma V. Cantu

The mission of the Office for Civil Rights is to ensure equal access to education and to promote educational excellence throughout the nation through vigorous enforcement of civil rights. A primary responsibility is resolving complaints of discrimination. Agency-initiated cases, typically called compliance reviews, permit OCR to target resources on compliance problems that appear particularly acute. OCR also provides technical assistance to help institutions achieve voluntary compliance with the civil rights laws that OCR enforces. In addition, OCR provides support to other Department of Education programs.

Office of Educational Research and Improvement (OERI)

U.S. Department of Education

OERI/At-Risk Room 610

555 New Jersey Avenue, NW

Washington, DC 20208-5521

Phone: (202) 219-2239

Fax: (202) 219-2030

Internet: http://www.ed.gov/offices/OERI/At-Risk
Contact: Holly Martinez, Acting Director
Phone: (202) 219-2239
E-mail: Debra_Hollinger_Martinez@ed.gov

The National Institute on the Education of At-Risk Students (At-Risk Institute) is one of five Institutes created by the Educational Research, Development, Dissemination and Improvement Act of 1994. These Institutes are located within the Office of Educational Research and Improvement at the U.S. Department of Education. The At-Risk Institute supports a range of research and development activities designed to improve the education of students at risk of educational failure because of limited English proficiency, poverty, race, geographic location, or economic disadvantage.

Office of Migrant Education

Internet: http://www.migranted.org

The Office of Migrant Education works to improve teaching and learning for migratory children. Programs and projects administered by OME are designed to enable children whose families migrate to find work in agricultural, fishing, and timber industries to meet the same challenging academic content and student performance standards that are expected of all children. The migrant education program is based on the premise that migrant children, although affected by poverty and the migrant lifestyle can and should have the opportunity to realize their full academic potential.

The goals of the Office of Migrant Education are as follows:

- *To improve coordination among all states to help improve educational outcomes for migrant children.*
- *To foster partnerships between State directors, federal agencies, and other organizations in order to improve coordination of services to migrant families.*

- *To ensure that migrant children have access to services to assist in overcoming cultural and language barriers, health-related problems, and other challenges that place children at risk for completing their education.*

Department of Health and Human Services
Centers for Disease Control and Prevention
Office of the Director
Associate Director for Minority Health

Walter Williams, Associate Director, Minority Health

Phone: 404-639-7210

Contact: Corlis Voltz

E-mail: cav2@cdc.gov

Internet: http://www.cdc.gov/od/admh

The mission of the Office of the Associate Director for Minority Health is to improve the health of the African-American (Blacks, Asian-American/Pacific Islander, Hispanic American, and Native American/Alaska Native Citizens, and, where appropriate, similar ethnic/racial subgroups both in and out of the United States, through policy development and program analysis at CDC and ATSDR.

National Institutes of Health
NIH Office of Extramural Research

Minorities Training Programs

Internet: http://grants.nih.gov/training/minorities.htm

Offers links to organizations that offer grant money for minority-based research.

Department of Housing and Urban Development
Headquarters Program Office
Office of Fair Housing and Equal Opportunity

US Department of Housing and Urban Development

451 7th Street SW

Washington, DC 20410

Phone: (202) 401-0388 (HUD)

Internet: http://www.hud.gov/fhe/fheo.html

Contact: N. Mykl Asanti

E-mail: N._Mykl_Asanti@hud.gov

This office exists to *enforce the Fair Housing Act and other civil rights laws to ensure the right of equal housing opportunity and free and fair housing choice without discrimination based on race, color, religion, sex, national origin, disability or family composition.* Its stated goals are to:

1. *Reduce discrimination in housing by doubling the Title VIII case load by the end of 2000 through aggressive enforcement of civil rights and fair housing laws;*

2. *Promote geographic mobility for low-income and minority households;*

3. *Integrate fair housing plans into HUD's Consolidated Plans;*

4. *Further fair housing in other relevant programs of the Federal government; and*

5. *Promote substantial equivalency among state, local and community organizations involved in providing housing.*

Department of Justice
Office of General Council
Civil Rights Division

Office of the Assistant Attorney General

Acting Director: Bill Lann Lee

P.O. Box 65808

Washington, D.C. 20035-5808

Phone: (202) 514-4609

Fax: (202) 514-0293

         (202) 307-2572

(202) 307-2839

Internet: http://www.usdoj.gov/crt/crt-home.html

The Civil Rights Division has served for the past 40 years as the federal government's chief guardian of the right of each and every person to live, learn, and work free from discrimination and threat of harm. The civil rights laws of the United States prohibit discrimination based on a number of factors -- including race, color, religion, sex, national origin, disability, age, familial status, citizenship status, marital status, and source of income -- in employment, education, public accommodations, housing, lending, programs receiving federal financial assistance, and in other areas.

Executive Office for Immigration Review

Public Affairs Office

5107 Leesburg Pike, Suite 2400

Falls Church, VA 22041

Phone: (703) 305-0289

Fax: (703) 605-0365

Internet: http://www.usdoj.gov/eoir

Under delegated authority of the Attorney General of the United States, EOIR administers and interprets Federal immigration laws and regulations through the conduct of immigration court proceedings, appellate reviews, and administrative hearings in individual cases. EOIR carries out these responsibilities through its three main components:

1. The Board of Immigration Appeals (BIA), which hears appeals of decisions made in individual cases by Immigration Judges, INS District Directors, or other immigration officials;

2. The Office of the Chief Immigration Judge (OCIJ), which oversees all the Immigration Courts and their proceedings throughout the United States; and

3. *The Office of the Chief Administrative Hearing Officer (OCAHO), which became part of EOIR in 1987 to resolve cases concerning employer sanctions, document fraud, and immigration-related employment discrimination.*

The purpose of these proceedings is to provide a process through which individuals can defend themselves against Government charges, complaints, or denials of benefits; or through which they can seek relief from penalties imposed against them. Every proceeding adheres to statutory and regulatory guidelines ensuring the uniform application of law and the fair and equitable treatment of all parties involved.

Department of State and Institute of International Education
Fulbright Program

IIE

809 United Nations Plaza

New York, NY 10017-3580

Internet: http://www.iie.org/fulbright

The Fulbright Program was established in 1946, at the end of World War II, to increase mutual understanding between the people of the United States and other countries, through the exchange of persons, knowledge, and skills. Grants are made to citizens of participating countries, primarily for:

- *university teaching;*
- *advanced research;*
- *graduate study; and*
- *teaching in elementary and secondary schools.*

Office of Undersecretary for Public Diplomacy and Public Affairs

Public Information, Rm. 6808

Bureau of Public Affairs

U.S. Department of State

Washington, DC 20520-6810

Phone: (202) 647-6575

(use this address for the bureaus listed below)

Bureau of Western Hemisphere Affairs

Internet: http://www.state.gov/www/regions/ara/index.html

The Bureau of Western Hemisphere Affairs, headed by Acting Assistant Secretary of State Peter F. Romero, is responsible for managing and promoting U.S. interests in the region by supporting democracy, trade, and sustainable economic development, and fostering cooperation on issues such as drug trafficking and crime, poverty reduction, and environmental protection.

Bureau of Educational and Cultural Affairs

Internet: http://e.usia.gov/education

The Bureau of Educational and Cultural Affairs (ECA) fosters mutual understanding between the United States and other countries through international educational and training programs. The bureau does so by promoting personal, professional, and institutional ties between private citizens and organizations in the United States and abroad, as well as by presenting U.S. history, society, art and culture in all of its diversity to overseas audiences.

Office of Undersecretary for Global Affairs
Bureau of Human Rights, Democracy, and Labor

Internet: http://www.state.gov/www/global/human_rights/index.html

This section of the DOS monitors human rights in other countries.

Bureau of Population, Refugees, and Migration

U.S. Department of State

2401 E Street, NW, Suite L-505, SA-1

Washington, D.C. 20522-0105

Internet: http://www.state.gov/www/global/prm/index.html

E-mail: prm@state.gov

Within the government, PRM has primary responsibility for formulating policies on population, refugees, and migration, and for administering U.S. refugee assistance and admissions programs. The Bureau is headed by Assistant Secretary of State Julia V. Taft, under the direction of the Under Secretary of State for Global Affairs.

With a $670 million budget, PRM administers and monitors U.S. contributions to international and non-governmental organizations to assist and protect refugees abroad. In overseeing admissions of refugees to the United States for permanent resettlement, the Bureau works closely with the Immigration and Naturalization Service, the Department of Health and Human Services, and various state and private voluntary agencies.

PRM coordinates U.S. international population policy and promotes its goals through bilateral and multilateral cooperation. It works closely with the U.S. Agency for International Development, which administers U.S. international population programs. The Bureau also coordinates U.S. international migration policy within the U.S. Government and through bilateral and multilateral diplomacy.

Environmental Protection Agency
Office of Civil Rights

1200 Pennsylvania Avenue, NW

Washington, DC 20004

Phone: (202) 260-4575

Fax: (202) 260-4580

Internet: http://www.epa.gov (EPA home)

Works to ensure, among other things, compliance with civil rights laws by recipients of EPA funds.

Environmental Protection Agency/ Secretaría de Medio Ambiente, Recursos Naturales y Pesca

U.S.-Mexico Border XXI/ Frontera XXI

E-mail: border.team@epa.gov

Internet: http://www.epa.gov/usmexicoborder

Joint US/ Mexico project that addresses environmental issues on the border. The Border XXI Program is a binational, interagency program aimed at protecting and improving the environment and environmental health while fostering sustainable development in the U.S.-Mexico border area.

Objectives which are central to the Border XXI Program include public involvement, decentralization of border decision making, and increased cooperation between the different governmental agencies operating in the border region.

Equal Employment Opportunity Commission

1801 L Street, NW

Washington, DC 20507

Phone: (202) 663-4900

Internet: http://www.eeoc.gov

Chairwoman: Ida A. Castro

Enforces civil rights laws as they pertain to hiring practices and workplace environment. The mission of the EEOC, as set forth in its strategic plan, is to promote equal opportunity in employment through administrative and judicial enforcement of the federal civil rights laws and through education and technical assistance.

The Inter-American Foundation

901 N. Stuart Street, 10th Floor

156

Arlington, VA 22203

Phone: (703) 306-4301

Fax: (703) 306-4365

Internet: http://www.iaf.gov

Independent federal agency concerned with economic development strategies in Western Hemisphere nations, particularly in Latin America and the Caribbean. *[I]t shall be the purpose of the Foundation, primarily in cooperation with private regional, and international organizations, to:*

1.Strengthen the bonds of friendship and understanding among the peoples of this hemisphere;

2.Support self-help efforts designed to enlarge the opportunities for individual development;

3.Stimulate and assist effective and ever wider participation of the people in the development process;

4.Encourage the establishment and growth of democratic institutions, private and governmental, appropriate to the requirements of the individual sovereign nations of this hemisphere.

Library of Congress
Reading Rooms

101 Independence Ave. SE

Washington, DC 20540

Phone: (202) 707-5000 or (202) 707-6500 (researchers' information)

Internet: http://lcweb.loc.gov/rr

Archives of various data, including African and Middle Eastern, Asian and genealogy.

Journals

Colonial Latin American Historical Review
Spanish Colonial Research Center, NPS
Zimmerman Library, University of New Mexico
Albuquerque, NM 87131
Phone: (505) 277-1370
Fax: (505) 277-4603
Internet: http://www.unm.edu/~clahr/
E-mail: clahr@unm.edu

CLAHR's objective is to promote the study of the colonial Luso-Hispano America and provide a greater understanding of the common heritage of North, Central, and South America and the Caribbean. Each issue...contains essays based on original research as well as book reviews and announcements of upcoming events.

Harvard Journal of Hispanic Policy
John F. Kennedy School of Government
Harvard University
79 John F. Kennedy Street
Cambridge, MA 02138
Phone: (617) 495-1311
Fax: (617) 496-9027
Internet: http://www.ksg.harvard.edu/hjhp/
E-mail: HJHP@ksg.harvard.edu

HJHP is a student-run, non-partisan, peer review publication that publishes interdisciplinary works on politics and policy making...[affecting] the Latino community in the United States. The Journal
serves as an information source for advocates and scholars serving the Latino community, as well as policy makers and practitioners at all levels of government.

Hispanic Journal
PO Box 810502
Dallas, TX 75381-0502
Phone: (214) 350-4774
Fax: (214) 358-0018
Internet: http://www.hispanicjournal.com/
E-mail: info@hispanicjournal.com

Latin American Perspectives
PO Box 5703
Riverside, CA 92517-5703
Phone: (909) 787-5037, ext. 1571
Fax: (909) 787-5685
Internet: http://wizard.ucr.edu/lap/lap.html
E-mail: laps@mail.ucr.edu

A theoretical and scholarly journal for discussion and debate on the political economy of capitalism, imperialism, and socialism in the Americas. ...the journal combines studies of economics, political science, international relations, philosophy, history, sociology, geography, anthropology and literature, into a comprehensive and scholarly examination of the current state of Latin America.

Letras Femeninas
Department of Modern Languages and Literatures
University of Nebraska – Lincoln

1111 Oldfather Hall
PO Box 880315
Lincoln, NE 68588-0316
Internet: http://www.unl.edu/modlang/journals/Letras/Letras.htm
Contact: Dr. Adelaida Martínez
E-mail: amartine@unlinfo.unl.edu

Journal of the *Asociación de Literatura Femenina Hispánica*. The journal *publishes critical and creative works providing extensive coverage of the scholarship in the literature of Hispanic women writers.*

Lucero: A Journal of Iberian and Latin American Studies

University of California, Berkeley
5319 Dwinelle Hall
Berkeley, CA 94720-2590
Phone: (510) 642-0471
Internet: http://socrates.berkeley.edu/~uclucero/
E-mail: uclucero@socrates.berkeley.edu

This literary journal, published by the graduate students of the Department of Spanish and Portuguese, accepts articles, book reviews, research, short stories and poetry.

V. Native-Americans

Libraries and Archival Resources

Alaska Native Language Center – Research Library
University of Alaska
302 Chapman Building
Fairbanks, AK 99701

Alaska and The Polar Regions Collection
University of Alaska
Elmer E. Rasmuston Library
Fairbanks, AK 99701

American Indian Historical Society – Library
1451 Masonic Ave.
San Francisco, CA 94117

Library and Archives
Cherokee National Historical Society, Inc.
Box 515
TSA-LA-G1
Tahlequah, OK 74464

Cherokee Regional Library
Georgia History and Geneaological Room
305 S. Duke St.
LaFayette, GA 30728

Chickasaw Council House Library
Oklahoma Historical Society

Court House Square

Tishomingo, OK 73460

Four Directions Educational Resource Library

Internet: http://www.4directions.org/index.html

Holds and categorizes curricular materials which have been contributed by educators of Native American students. [Materials] *are subject to a review process prior to being included in the databases.*

Gallup Indian Medical Center – Medical Library
U.S. Public Health Service Hospital

E. Nizhoni Blvd., Box 1337

Gallup, NM 84301

The George Gustav Heye Center
Alexander Hamilton U.S. Custom House

One Bowling Green

New York, NY 10004

Phone: (212) 514-3737

Dedicated to preservation, study, and exhibition of the life, languages, literature, history, and art of Native Americans, the museum works in collaboration with the Native Americans to protect and foster their cultures. Collections span more than 10,000 years of Native heritage: 70% of one million objects in collections represent cultures in the United States and Canada; 30% represent cultures in Mexico and Central and South America.

The Heard Museum - Library and Archives

22 E. Monte Vista Rd.

Phoenix, AZ 85004

Phone: (602) 252-8840

Fax: (602) 252-9757

Hours: 10am-4:45pm, M-F

This private, non-profit museum, founded in 1929, *promotes appreciation and respect for Native people and their cultural heritage, with emphasis on the traditional cultures of the Greater Southwest and on enhancing the Native-American Fine Art movement.* Their non-lending reference collection is located on the 2nd floor. An appointment is necessary to use archival collections and audiovisual materials.

Library of Congress – American Folklife Center

Thomas Jefferson Building, G1040

Washington, DC 20540

Museum of Indian Heritage – Library

Eagle Creek Park

6040 DeLong Rd.

Indianapolis, IN 46254

National Indian Education Association – Library

Ivy Tower Building, 2nd Floor

1115 2nd Ave. S.

Minneapolis, MN 55403

National Museum of the American Indian

Smithsonian Institute

Executive offices: 470 L'Enfant Plaza, SW, Ste.7102

Washington, DC 20560

Native American Studies Library

University of California, Berkeley
343 Dwinelle Hall
Berkeley, CA 94720

Navajo Nation Library
Box K
Window Rock, AZ 86515

Pacific Northwest Collection
University of Washington – Special Collections Division
Suzzallo Library, FM-25
Seattle, WA 98195

Ponca City Cultural Center Museum – Library
1000 E. Grand St.
Ponca City, OK 74601

Resource Center - National Museum of the American Indian
George Gustav Heye Center
Internet: http://www.conexus.si.edu
Phone: (212) 514-3799

The main reference center for NMAI. Annotated bibliographies available upon request.

Popular Media

Film and Video Center
National Museum of the American Indian
George Gustav Heye Center

Phone: (212) 514-3737

E-mail: fvc@ic.si.edu

Dedicated to public programs and information services concerning film, video, radio, and electronic media by and about indigenous peoples of North, Central, and South America and Hawaii. Media collection houses 1500 titles. A selection of 250 videotapes is available for viewing without appointment in the museum's Resource Center. Museum does not sell or lend films and video.

Colleges/Universities
(from U.S. Office of Civil Rights)

Bay Mills Community College
Martha McLeod, President
12214 West Lake Shore Drive
Brimley, MI 49715
Phone: (906) 248-3354
Fax: (906) 248-3351
E-mail: mmcleod@bmcc.org

Blackfeet Community College
Carol Murray, President
P.O. Box 819
Browning, MT 59417
Phone: (406) 338-7755
Fax: (406) 338-3272

Cankdeska Cikana Community College
Erich Longie, President
P.O. Box 269

Fort Totten, ND 58335

Phone: (701) 766-4415

Fax: (701) 766-4077

E-mail: ericstev@hoopster.little-hoop.cc.nd.us

Cheyenne River Community College

Mike McCafferty, President

P.O. Box 220

Eagle Butte, SD 57625

Phone: (605) 964-6044

Fax: (605) 964-1144

E-mail: jgarrett@rapidnet.com

College of the Menominee Nation

Dr. Verna Fowler, President

P.O. Box 1179

Keshena, WI 54135

Phone: (715) 799-4921

Fax: (715) 799-1308

Internet: http://www.menominee.com

E-mail: vfowler@menominee.com

Crownpoint Institute of Technology

James Tutt, President

P.O. Box 849

Crownpoint, NM 87313

Phone: (505) 786-5851

Fax: (505) 786-5644

E-mail: jmtutt@aol.com

D-Q University

Dr. Morgan Otis, President
P.O. Box 409
Davis, CA 95617
Phone: (916) 758-0470
Fax: (916) 758-4891
E-mail: motis@daq.cc.ca.us

Founded in 1971, the only accredited, private Native-American institution of higher learning in California. Emphasizes basics such as language and mathematics while drawing on the strength of Native-American cultures. Offers associates' degrees and certificates.

Diné College

Dr. Tommy Lewis, President
P.O. Box 126
Tsaile, AZ 86556
Phone: (520) 724-6669
Fax: (520) 724-3327
E-mail: tlewis@crystal.ncc.cc.nm.us

Dull Knife Memorial College

Alonzo Spang, President
P.O. Box 98
Lame Deer, MT 59043
Phone: (406) 477-6215
Fax: (406) 477-6219
E-mail: aspang@dkmc.cc.mt.us

Fond du Lac Tribal and Community College

Lester Jack Briggs, President
2101 14th Street

Cloquet, MN 55720-2964

Phone: (218) 879-0800

Fax: (218) 879-0814

E-mail: ljbriggs@asab.fdl.cc.mn.us

gopher://gopher.fdl.cc.mn.us

Fort Belknap College

Dr. Philip Shortman, President

P.O. Box 159

Harlem, MT 59526

Phone: (406) 353-2607

Fax: (406) 353-2898

E-mail: tshortbull@dc.edu.com

Fort Berthold Community College

Elizabeth Yellowbird Demeray, Acting President

P.O. Box 490

New Town, ND 58763

Phone: (701) 627-4738

Fax: (701) 627-3609

E-mail: ldemeray@nt1.fort-berthold.cc.nd.us

Fort Peck Community College

Dr. James Shanley, President

P.O. Box 398

Poplar, MT 59255

Phone: (406) 768-5551

Fax: (406) 768-5552

E-mail: jimsh@fpcc.cc.mt.us

Haskell Indian Nations University

Dr. Robert Martin, President

155 Indian Ave, Box 5030

Lawrence, KS 66046-4800

Phone: (785) 749-8497

Fax: (785) 749-8411

E-mail: bmartin@ross1.cc.haskell.edu

Lac Courte Oreilles Ojibwa Community College

Dr. Jasjit Minhas, President

R.R. 2, Box 2357

Hayward, WI 54843

Phone: (715) 634-4790

Fax: (715) 634-5049

E-mail: lcoocc1@win.bright.net

Leech Lake Tribal College

Larry Aitken, President

Rt. 3, Box 100

Cass Lake, MN 56633

Phone: (218) 335-2828

Fax: (218) 335-7845

E-mail: larry@paulbunyan.net

Little Big Horn College

Dr. Janine Pease-Pretty on Top, President

P.O. Box 370

Crow Agency, MT 59022

Phone: (406) 638-2228

Fax: (406) 638-2229

E-mail: janine@main1.lbhc.cc.mt.us

Little Priest Tribal College

John Blackhawk, President

P.O. Box 270

Winnebago, NE 68071

Phone: (402) 878-2380

Fax: (402) 878-2355

E-mail: jwb@lptc.cc.ne.us

Nebraska Indian Community College

Schuyler Houser, President

P.O. Box 164

Niobrara, NE 68760

Phone: (402) 857-2434

Fax: (402) 857-2543

E-mail: sky708@aol.com

Northwest Indian College

Dr. Robert Lorence, President

2522 Kwina Road

Bellingham, WA 98226

Phone: (360) 676-2772

Fax: (360) 738-0136

E-mail: blorence@nwic.edu

Oglala Lakota College

Thomas Shortbull, President

P.O. Box 490

Kyle, SD 57752

Phone: (605) 455-2321

Fax: (605) 455-2787

Salish Kootenai College

Dr. Joe McDonald, President

P.O. Box 117

Pablo, MT 59855

Phone: (406) 675-4800

Fax: (406) 675-4801

E-mail: j_mcdonald@skc.edu , or anita_bigspring@skc.edu

Sinte Gleska University

Dr. Lionel Bordeaux, President

P.O. Box 490

Rosebud, SD 57570

Phone: (605) 747-2263

Fax: (605) 747-2098

Sisseton Wahpeton Community College

Elden Lawrence, President

P.O. Box 689

Sisseton, SD 57262

Phone: (605) 698-3966

Fax: (605) 698-3132

E-mail: elden@daknet.com

Sitting Bull College

Ron McNeil, President

HC1, Box 4

Fort Yates, ND 58338

Phone: (701) 854-3861

Fax: (701) 854-3403

E-mail: rsmcneil@aol.com

Southwestern Indian Polytechnic Institute

Dr. Carolyn Elgin, President

P.O. Box 10146-9169

Coors Road, NW

Albuquerque, NM 87184

Phone: (505) 897-5347

Fax: (505) 897-5343

E-mail: ce@native.sipi.bia.edu

Stone Child College

Steve Galbavy, President

Rocky Boy Rt. Box 1082

Box Elder, MT 59521

Phone: (406) 395-4313

Fax: (406) 395-4836

E-mail: steve@sccrockyboy.org

Turtle Mountain Community College

Dr. Carty Monette, President

P.O. Box 340

Belcourt, ND 58316

Phone: (701) 477-5605

Fax: (701) 477-5028

E-mail: cartym@aol.com

United Tribes Technical College

Dr. David Gipp, President

3315 University Drive

Bismarck, ND 58504

Phone: (701) 255-3285

Fax: (701) 530-0605

E-mail: dmgipp@aol.com

White Earth Tribal and Community College
Helen Klassen, President
202 Main Street South
P.O. Box 478
Mahnomen, MN 56557
Phone: (218) 935-0417
Fax: (218) 935-0423

Xavier University of Louisiana
7325 Palmetto St.
New Orleans, LA 70125
Phone: (504) 486-7411 or (504) 483-7308
Fax: (504) 485-7941
E-mail: apply@xula.edu

- private university affiliated with the Catholic Church, founded in 1915 to serve Native and African Americans
- library Resource Center houses over 200,000 titles, 1100 periodical and newspaper subscriptions, and 100,000 microfilms
- over 50% of student body enrolled in natural sciences
- approximately 3500 enrolled
- student/faculty ratio: 14:1

Special Programs

(from the Online Guide to Native American Studies Programs, edited by Robert M. Nelson)

Alaska Native Studies
University of Alaska, Fairbanks
PO Box 756300
Fairbanks, AK 99775-6300
Phone: (907) 474-7181
Contact: Phyllis A. Fast

Offers a BA major and minor.

American Indian Studies
University of Arizona
PO Box 210076
Harvill 430
Tucson, AZ 85721-0076
Phone: (520) 621-7108
Internet: http://w3.arizona.edu/~aisp/
Contact: Jay Stauss

Offers an MA, PhD, and a concurrent MA/JD degree in American Indian Studies and Law.

Indian Studies Program
Bemidji State University
1500 Birchmont Dr. NE
Bemidji, MN 56601

Phone: (218) 755-3977

Internet: http://www.bemidji.msus.edu/bsucatalog/INST/Index.html

Contact: Kent Smith

Offers a BA major and minor in Indian Studies and a minor in Ojibwe language.

Native American Studies
University of California, Berkeley
506 Barrows Hall

Berkeley, CA 94720-2570

Phone: (510) 642-6717

Internet: http://socrates.berkeley.edu/~ethnicst/

Contact: Gerald Vizenor

Offers a BA major in Native American Studies and a PhD in Ethnic Studies with a concentration in Native American Studies.

Native American Studies
University of California, Davis
Dept. of Native American Studies

Davis, CA 95616

Phone: (916) 752-3237

Internet: http://cougar.ucdavis.edu/nas/

Contact: Ines Hernandez-Avila

Offers a BA major and minor, MA and PhD in Native American Studies, and an emphasis in Native American Studies at the MA and PhD levels.

Interdepartmental Program in American Indian Studies
University of California, Los Angeles
3220 Campbell

Box 951548

Los Angeles, CA 90095-1548

Phone: (910) 206-7511

Internet: http://www.sscnet.ucla.edu/indian/IDPHome.html

Contact: Dwight Youpee

Offers an MA in American Indian Studies and a MA/JD in Law.

Indigenous Peoples of the Americas Program
Colby College

Dept. of English

Colby College

Waterville, ME 04901

Phone: (207) 872-3292

Contact: Pat Onion

Offers an interdisciplinary minor.

Native American Studies
Colgate University

Dept. of English

Hamilton, NY 13346

Phone: (315) 228-7781

Internet: http://www2.colgate.edu/departments/soan/

Contact: Sarah A. Wilder

Offers a major, minor and concentration in Native American Studies.

Individualized Major in Native American Studies
University of Connecticut

Native American Studies Office

Room 322, Box U-158

Manchester Hall

University of Connecticut

Storrs, CT 06269-2158

Phone: (860) 486-4512 or (860) 486-4511

E-mail: bee@uconnvm.uconn.edu

Contact: Robert L. Bee

Offers a BA in Native American Studies

American Indian Program

Cornell University

300 Caldwell Hall

Ithaca, NY 14853

Phone: (607) 255-6587

Internet: http://www.aip.cornell.edu/

Contact: Jane Mt. Pleasant

Offers an undergraduate concentration and a graduate minor in American Indian Studies

Native American Studies

Dartmouth College

Sherman House

37 N. Main St. HB 6152

Hanover, NH 03755

Phone: (603) 646-3530

Internet: http://www.dartmouth.edu/~nas/

Contact: Colin G. Calloway

Offers a BA major and minor.

American Indian Studies
University of Denver
University College
2211 S. Josephine St.
Denver, CO 80210
Phone: (303) 871-3155
Internet: http://www.du.edu/ucol/ais/
E-mail: ucolinfo@du.edu
Contact: John Compton

Offers a Master of Liberal Studies with a concentration in American History and Cultures and a Certificate of Advanced Study in American Indian History and Cultures.

American Indian Studies
Five Colleges, Inc.
PO Box 740
97 Spring St.
Amherst, MA 01004
Internet: http://www.fivecolleges.edu
E-mail: ntherien@amherst.edu
Contact: Nate Therien

Offers a Native Studies certificate program for BA and B.S. on the campuses of University of Massachusetts, Amherst College, Hampshire College, Smith College, and Mount Holyoke College.

Native American Studies
Humboldt State University
Ethnic Studies

Arcata, CA 95521

Phone: (707) 826-4329

Contact: Victor Golla

Offers a BA major and minor.

Native American Studies Program
University of Maine

5724 Dunn Hall

University of Maine

Orono, ME 04469

Phone: (207) 581-1417

Internet: http://www.umaine.edu/wabanaki/n

Contact: Dr. Maureen E. Smith

Offers an interdisciplinary minor.

American Indian Studies
University of Minnesota, Twin Cities

107 Scott Hall

72 Pleasant St. SE

Minneapolis, MN 55455

Phone: (612) 624-1338

Internet: http://cla.umn.edu/amerind/amin.html

Contact: Patricia Albers

Offers a BA major and minor.

Native American Studies
University of Montana

600 University Ave.

Missoula, MT 59812

Phone: (406) 243-5831

Internet: http://www.umt.edu/nas/

Contact: Larry LaCounte

Offers BA major and minor.

Native American Studies

University of Nebraska at Omaha

College of Arts and Sciences

Omaha, NE 68182-0150

Phone: (402) 554-3379

Internet: http://www.unomaha.edu/Uno/arts-science.html

Contact: Bruce E. Johansen

Offers an undergraduate minor and both a BA and MA in Interdisciplinary Studies with an emphasis on Native American Studies.

Native American Studies

University of New Mexico

Mesa Vista Hall, Room 3080, 3rd Floor

Albuquerque, NM 87131

Phone: (505) 277-3917

Internet: http://www.unm.edu/~nasinfo/

Contact: Lee Francis

Offers an undergraduate Interdisciplinary Specialization Certificate in Native American Studies.

American Indian Studies

University of North Carolina at Pembroke

PO Box 1510

Pembroke, NC 28372-1510

Phone: (910) 521-6266 or (800) 822-2185

Internet: http://www.uncp.edu/catalog/aisprograms.htm

Contact: Dr. Linda E. Oxendine

Offers a BA major, minor or concentration.

Native American Studies
State University of New York at Buffalo

1010A Clemens Hall

Buffalo, NY 14260

Phone: (715) 645-2546

Internet: http://wings.buffalo.edu/academic/department/AandL/ams/

Contact: Oren Lyons

Offers a BA in American Studies with a concentration in Native American Studies.

American Indian Studies Program
University of Wisconsin, Eau Claire

Box 4004

Eau Claire, WI 54702

Phone: (715) 836-6045 or (715) 836-3243

Internet: http://www.uwec.edu/Academic/AIS/

Contact: Dr. Lawrence Martin

Offers BA major and minor.

American Indian Studies Program
University of Wisconsin, Madison

317 Ingraham Hall
1155 Observatory Dr.
Madison, WI 53706
Phone: (608) 263-5501
Fax: (608) 262-7137
Internet: http://polyglot.1ss.wisc.edu/aisp
Contact: Roberta Hill

Offers a Certificate in American Indian Studies.

American Indian Studies
University of Wyoming
PO Box 3431
Laramie, WY 82071-3431
Phone: (307) 766-6521
Internet: http://www.wyo.edu/a&s/aist/index.htm
E-mail: antell@uwyo.edu
Contact: Dr. Judith Antell

Offers a BA minor.

Special Centers

American Indian Studies Center
University of Washington
Box 354305
Seattle, WA 98195
Phone: (206) 543-9082
Internet: http://www.washington.edu/students/gencat/academic/amerindian.html
Contact: Dr. Thomas Colonesse

Offers an undergraduate minor and a BA in Anthropology with an emphasis in American Indian Studies.

Center for Native American Studies
Montana State University
Wilson Hall 2-152
Bozeman, MT 59717-0346
Phone: (406) 994-3881
Contact: Dr. Wayne Stein

Offers an interdisciplinary program of study, possibly leading to a minor.

Center for Native American and World Indigenous Peoples Studies
The Evergreen State College
Olympia, WA 98505
Phone: (360) 866-6000
Contact: Alan Parker

Offers full-time interdisciplinary programs in conjunction with the Northwest Indian College. Works closely with community colleges on seven reservations.

The Indian Cultural and Resource Center
American Indian Studies Department
College of St. Scholastica
1200 Kenwood Ave.
Duluth, MN 55811-4199
Phone: (218) 723-6170
Internet: http://www.css.edu/depts/amind.html

Institute of American Indian and Alaska Native Culture and Arts Development

PO Box 20007, St. Michael's Drive

Santa Fe, NM 87504

Phone: (505) 988-6463

Fax: (505) 988-6446

Internet: http://www.iaiancad.org

President: Beatrice Rivas Sanchez

- the Institute's mission is to *serve as a multi-tribal Native center of higher education for Native Americans*
- public, 2-year school

Josephine White Eagle Cultural Center

University of Massachusetts

Amherst, MA 01003

Internet: http://www-unix.oit.umass.edu/~deervinc/

Contains a computer lab, study hall and library.

Government Programs

American Indian Higher Education Consortium

121 Oronoco Street

Alexandria, VA 22314

Phone: (703) 838-0400

Fax: (703) 838-0388

E-mail: aihec@aihec.org

Commission on Civil Rights
624 9th Street, NW
Washington, D.C. 20425
Western Regional Office
Suite 810
3660 Wilshire Boulevard
Los Angeles, California 90010
Contact: Philip Montez, Director
Phone: (213) 894-3437
Internet: http://www.usccr.gov

The U.S. Commission on Civil Rights is an independent, bipartisan agency first established by Congress in 1957 and reestablished in 1983. It is directed to:

- *Investigate complaints alleging that citizens are being deprived of their right to vote by reason of their race, color, religion, sex, age, disability, or national origin, or by reason of fraudulent practices;*
- *Study and collect information relating to discrimination or a denial of equal protection of the laws under the Constitution because of race, color, religion, sex, age, disability, or national origin, or in the administration of justice;*
- *Appraise Federal laws and policies with respect to discrimination or denial of equal protection of the laws because of race, color, religion, sex, age, disability, or national origin, or in the administration of justice;*
- *Serve as a national clearinghouse for information in respect to discrimination or denial of equal protection of the laws because of race, color, religion, sex, age, disability, or national origin;*
- *Submit reports, findings, and recommendations to the President and Congress;*
- *Issue public service announcements to discourage discrimination or denial of equal protection of the laws.*

Department of Commerce
Census Bureau

American Fact Finder

Internet: http://factfinder.census.gov/java_prod/dads.ui.homePage.HomePage

Provides information from 1990 census in a variety of forms. Allows the user to create profiles of almost any American community or region based on demographics data such as income and more.

Minority Business Development Agency

14th St. & Constitution Ave., NW

Room 5055

Washington, DC 20230

Internet: http://www.mbda.gov

Feedback Form: http://www.mbda.gov/contact.asp

The Minority Business Development Agency (MBDA), is part of the U.S. Department of Commerce. MBDA is the only Federal Agency created specifically to foster the creation, growth and expansion of minority-owned businesses in America.

Department of Education
Office of Bilingual Education and Minority Languages Affairs

600 Independence Avenue, SW

Washington, DC 20202-6510

Internet: http://www.ed.gov/offices/OBEMLA

E-mail: askncbe@ncbe.gwu.edu

Contact: Art Love, Acting Director

Phone: (202) 205-5463

E-mail: art_love@ed.gov

Congress passed the Bilingual Education Act in 1968 in recognition of the growing number of linguistically and culturally diverse children enrolled in schools who, because of their limited English proficiency, were not receiving an education equal to their English-proficient peers. The purpose of this Act was, and continues to be, aligned with Title VI of the Civil Rights Act of 1964 which the Department interprets as follows:

Where inability to speak and understand the English language excludes national origin minority group children from effective participation in the educational program offered by a school district, the district must take affirmative steps to rectify the language deficiency in order to open its instructional program to these students.

Established in 1974 by Congress, the Office of Bilingual Education and Minority Languages Affairs helps school districts meet their responsibility to provide equal education opportunity to limited English proficient children.

Office for Civil Rights

Customer Service Team

Mary E. Switzer Building

330 C Street, SW

Washington, DC 20202

Phone: (202) 205-5413; 1-800-421-3481

Fax: (202) 205-9862

Internet: http://www.ed.gov/offices/OCR

E-mail: OCR@ED.Gov

Assistant Secretary Office of Civil Rights: Norma V. Cantú

The mission of the Office for Civil Rights is to ensure equal access to education and to promote educational excellence throughout the nation through vigorous enforcement of civil rights. A primary responsibility is resolving complaints of discrimination. Agency-initiated cases, typically called compliance reviews, permit OCR to target resources on compliance problems that appear particularly acute. OCR also provides technical assistance to help institutions achieve voluntary compliance with the civil rights laws that OCR enforces. In addition, OCR provides support to other Department of Education programs.

Office of Educational Research and Improvement (OERI)

U.S. Department of Education

OERI/At-Risk Room 610

555 New Jersey Avenue, NW

Washington, DC 20208-5521

Phone: (202) 219-2239

Fax: (202) 219-2030

Internet: http://www.ed.gov/offices/OERI/At-Risk

Contact: Holly Martinez, Acting Director

Phone: (202) 219-2239

E-mail: Debra_Hollinger_Martinez@ed.gov

The National Institute on the Education of At-Risk Students (At-Risk Institute) is one of five Institutes created by the Educational Research, Development, Dissemination and Improvement Act of 1994. These Institutes are located within the Office of Educational Research and Improvement at the U.S. Department of Education. The At-Risk Institute supports a range of research and development activities designed to improve the education of students at risk of educational failure because of limited English proficiency, poverty, race, geographic location, or economic disadvantage.

Office of Elementary and Secondary Education
Office of Indian Education Programs

Internet: http://www.ed.gov/offices/OESE/indian.html

Director: David Beaulieu

Under Title IX of the Elementary and Secondary Education Act of 1965 (ESEA), Indian education programs are authorized to support the efforts of local educational agencies, Indian tribes, and other entities to meet the special educational and culturally related academic needs of American Indians and Alaska Natives. The programs include: formula grants to local educational agencies, covering a range of supplemental activities for targeted youth; demonstration programs for improving educational opportunities for Indian Children; professional development programs for increasing the number of Indian individuals in designated professions; a fellowship program for undergraduate and graduate study; programs for the gifted and talented and adult education; and national research activities.

Primary functions of the Indian Education office include:

- *Grants Management - Design and oversee system for administering all types of Indian education grants including formula, discretionary, and fellowships.*
- *Evaluation - Prepare and track performance indicators and help coordinate national evaluations of programs.*
- *Administration - Provide routine administrative support for correspondence, mass mailing, telephone response.*
- *Intra agency Coordination - Provide leadership for ED-wide policy coordination in Indian Education formulating policy and guidance and identifying key issue areas.*
- *Interagency Coordination - Maintain working relationships with other agencies affecting Indian Education, particularly the Bureau of Indian Affairs.*
- *Communication - Help develop and implement a system for maintaining open communications with the field including a strong relationship with NACIE.*

Office of Migrant Education

Internet: http://www.migranted.org

The Office of Migrant Education works to improve teaching and learning for migratory children. Programs and projects administered by OME are designed to enable children whose families migrate to find work in agricultural, fishing, and timber industries to meet the same challenging academic content and student performance standards that are expected of all children. The migrant education program is based on the premise that migrant children, although affected by poverty and the migrant lifestyle can and should have the opportunity to realize their full academic potential.

The goals of the Office of Migrant Education are as follows:

- *To improve coordination among all states to help improve educational outcomes for migrant children.*

- *To foster partnerships between State directors, federal agencies, and other organizations in order to improve coordination of services to migrant families.*

- *To ensure that migrant children have access to services to assist in overcoming cultural and language barriers, health-related problems, and other challenges that place children at risk for completing their education.*

Department of Health and Human Services
Centers for Disease Control and Prevention
Office of the Director
Associate Director for Minority Health

Walter Williams, Associate Director, Minority Health

Phone: 404-639-7210

Contact: Corlis Voltz

E-mail: cav2@cdc.gov

Internet: http://www.cdc.gov/od/admh

The mission of the Office of the Associate Director for Minority Health is to improve the health of the African-American (Blacks, Asian-American/Pacific Islander, Hispanic American, and Native American/Alaska Native Citizens, and, where appropriate, similar ethnic/racial subgroups both in and out of the United States, through policy development and program analysis at CDC and ATSDR.

Indian Health Service

Communications Staff, Indian Health Service

Room 6-35, Parklawn Building, 5600 Fishers Lane

Rockville, MD 20857

Phone: (301) 443-3593

Fax: (301) 443-0507

Internet: http://www.ihs.gov

The Indian Health Service (I H S), an agency within the U S Department of Health and Human Services, is responsible for providing federal health services to American Indians and Alaska Natives. The provision of health services to members of federally recognized tribes grew out of the special government to government relationship between the United States federal government and Indian tribes. This relationship, established in 1787, is based on Article I, Section 8 of the Constitution, and has been given form and s*ubstance by numerous treaties, laws, Supreme Court decisions, and Executive Orders.*

The I H S is the principal federal health care provider and health advocate for Indian people, and its goal is to assure that comprehensive, culturally acceptable personal and public health services are available and accessible to American Indian and Alaska Native people. The I H S currently provides health services to approximately 1.5 million American Indians and Alaska Natives who belong to more than 550 federally recognized tribes in 35 states.

Department of Housing and Urban Development
Headquarters Program Office
Office of Fair Housing and Equal Opportunity

US Department of Housing and Urban Development

451 7th Street SW

Washington, DC 20410

Phone: (202) 401-0388 (HUD)

Internet: http://www.hud.gov/fhe/fheo.html

Contact: N. Mykl Asanti

E-mail: N._Mykl_Asanti@hud.gov

This office exists to *enforce the Fair Housing Act and other civil rights laws to ensure the right of equal housing opportunity and free and fair housing choice without discrimination based on race, color, religion, sex, national origin, disability or family composition.* Its stated goals are to:

1. *Reduce discrimination in housing by doubling the Title VIII case load by the end of 2000 through aggressive enforcement of civil rights and fair housing laws;*

2. *Promote geographic mobility for low-income and minority households;*

3. *Integrate fair housing plans into HUD's Consolidated Plans;*

4. *Further fair housing in other relevant programs of the Federal government; and*

5. *Promote substantial equivalency among state, local and community organizations involved in providing housing.*

Office of Public and Indian Housing

Assistant Secretary for Public and Indian Housing

451 7th Street, SW

Room 4100

Washington, DC 20410

Phone: (202) 401-0388 (HUD)

Contact: Harold Lucas, Assistant Secretary

Phone: (202) 708-0950

Internet: http://www.hud.gov/pih/pih.html

Our aim is to ensure safe, decent, and affordable housing; create opportunities for residents' self-sufficiency and economic independence; and assure fiscal integrity by all program participants. In order to achieve this mission, we will:

- *Recognize the residents as our ultimate customer*
- *Improve, PHA management and service delivery efforts through oversight, assistance, and selective intervention by highly skilled, diagnostic, and results-oriented field personnel*
- *Seek problem-solving partnerships with PHA, resident, community, and government leadership*
- *Act as a agent for change when performance is unacceptable and we judge that local leadership is not capable or committed to improvement*
- *Efficiently apply limited HUD resources by using risk assessment techniques to focus our oversight efforts*

Department of the Interior
Assistant Secretary – Indian Affairs
Bureau of Indian Affairs

Office of Public Affairs MS-4245 MIB

1849 C Street, NW

Washington, DC 20240-0001

Phone: (202) 208-3711

Fax: (202) 501-1516

Internet: http://www.doi.gov/bureau-indian-affairs.html

The Bureau of Indian Affairs' mission is to enhance the quality of life, to promote economic opportunity, and to carry out the responsibility to protect and improve the trust assets of American Indians, Indian tribes and Alaska Natives. We will accomplish this through the delivery of quality services, maintaining government-to-government relationships within the spirit of Indian self-determination. The BIA administers various programs to these ends.

Indian Arts and Crafts Board

1849 C Street, NW, MS 4004-MIB

Washington, DC 20240

Phone: (202) 208-3773

Fax: (202) 208-5196

Internet: http://www.doi.gov/iacb

This group promotes Native American and Native Alaskan economic development. *A top priority of the Board is the implementation and enforcement of the Indian Arts and Crafts Act of 1990, a truth-in-advertising law that provides criminal and civil penalties for marketing products as "Indian-made" when such products are not made by Indians, as defined by the Act. The Board's other activities include providing professional business advice, information on the Act and related marketing issues, fundraising assistance, and promotional opportunities to Native American artists, craftspeople, and cultural organizations.*

Assistant Secretary--Fish and Wildlife and Parks
National Park Service
American Indian Liaison Office

National Park Service (2205)

1849 C St. NW Rm. 3410

Washington, D.C. 20240

Phone: (202) 208-5475

Fax: (202) 273-0870

Internet: http://www.cr.nps.gov/ailo/ailohome.htm

Contact: Patricia L. Parker, Chief

E-mail: Pat_Parker@nps.gov

Created in February 1995, as part of the National Park Service Restructuring Plan, this office reports directly to the Associate Director, Cultural Resource Stewardship and Partnerships.

MISSION STATEMENT

To improve relationships between American Indian Tribes, Alaska Natives, Native Hawaiians and the National Park Service through consultation, outreach, technical assistance, education, and advisory services.

Office of the Secretary
Office of the Special Trustee for American Indians

U.S. Department of the Interior

1849 C Street, NW

Washington, DC 20240

Phone: (202) 208-3100

Internet: http://www.ost.doi.gov

Established by the American Indian Trust Fund Management Reform Act of 1994 (PL 103-412), the Office of the Special Trustee for American Indians (OST) was created to improve the accountability and management of Indian funds held in trust by the federal government. As trustee, the Department of the Interior has the primary fiduciary responsibility to manage both Tribal trust funds and Individual Indian Monies (IIM) accounts.

Department of Justice
Office of General Council
Civil Rights Division

Office of the Assistant Attorney General

Acting Director: Bill Lann Lee

P.O. Box 65808

Washington, D.C. 20035-5808

Phone: (202) 514-4609

Fax: (202) 514-0293, (202) 307-2572 or (202) 307-2839

Internet: http://www.usdoj.gov/crt/crt-home.html

The Civil Rights Division has served for the past 40 years as the federal government's chief guardian of the right of each and every person to live, learn, and work free from discrimination and threat of harm. The civil rights laws of the United States prohibit discrimination based on a number of factors -- including race, color, religion, sex, national origin, disability, age, familial status, citizenship status, marital status, and source of income -- in employment, education, public accommodations, housing, lending, programs receiving federal financial assistance, and in other areas.

Office of Justice Programs
American Indian & Alaskan Native Affairs Desk

Office of Justice Programs
810 Seventh Street, NW
Washington, DC 20531
Phone: (202) 307-0703

The American Indian and Alaska Native (AI/AN) Affairs Desk has been established in the Office of Justice Programs (OJP), in the U.S. Department of Justice (DOJ) to enhance access to information by Federally recognized American Indian and Alaska Native tribes regarding funding opportunities, training and technical assistance, and other relevant information. Additionally, the American Indian & Alaska Native Affairs Desk coordinates with the Office of Tribal Justice on department wide AI/AN initiatives.

Department of State and Institute of International Education
Fulbright Program

IIE
809 United Nations Plaza
New York, NY 10017-3580
Internet: http://www.iie.org/fulbright

The Fulbright Program was established in 1946, at the end of World War II, to increase mutual understanding between the people of the United States and other countries, through the exchange of persons, knowledge, and skills. Grants are made to citizens of participating countries, primarily for:

- *university teaching;*
- *advanced research;*
- *graduate study; and*
- *teaching in elementary and secondary schools.*

Environmental Protection Agency
Office of Civil Rights
1200 Pennsylvania Avenue, NW

Washington, DC 20004

Phone: (202) 260-4575

Fax: (202) 260-4580

Internet: http://www.epa.gov (EPA home)

This division works to ensure, among other things, compliance with civil rights laws by recipients of EPA funds.

Office of Water
American Indian Environmental Office
Washington, DC

Internet: http://www.epa.gov/indian

Director: Kathy Gorospe

Phone: (202) 260-7939

Intra-agency program that exists to ensure protection of tribal lands. *The American Indian Environmental Office (AIEO) coordinates the Agency-wide effort to strengthen public health and environmental protection in Indian Country, with a special emphasis on building Tribal capacity to administer their own environmental programs. AIEO oversees development and implementation of the Agency's Indian Policy and strives to ensure that all EPA Headquarters and Regional Offices implement their parts of the Agency's Indian Program in a manner consistent with Administration policy to work with Tribes on a government-to-government basis and EPA's trust responsibility to protect Tribal health and environments.*

Environmental Protection Agency/ Secretaría de Medio Ambiente, Recursos Naturales y Pesca

U.S.-Mexico Border XXI/ Frontera XXI

E-mail: border.team@epa.gov

Internet: http://www.epa.gov/usmexicoborder

Joint US/ Mexico project that addresses environmental issues on the border. The Border XXI Program is a binational, interagency program aimed at protecting and improving the environment and environmental health while fostering sustainable development in the U.S.-Mexico border area.

Objectives which are central to the Border XXI Program include public involvement, decentralization of border decision making, and increased cooperation between the different governmental agencies operating in the border region.

Equal Employment Opportunity Commission

1801 L Street, NW

Washington, DC 20507

Phone: (202) 663-4900

Internet: http://www.eeoc.gov

Chairwoman: Ida A. Castro

Enforces civil rights laws as they pertain to hiring practices and workplace environment. The mission of the EEOC, as set forth in its strategic plan, is to promote equal opportunity in employment through administrative and judicial enforcement of the federal civil rights laws and through education and technical assistance.

Library of Congress
Reading Rooms
101 Independence Ave. SE

Washington, DC 20540

Phone: (202) 707-5000 or (202) 707-6500 (researchers' information)

Internet: http://lcweb.loc.gov/rr

These are archives of various data, including African and Middle Eastern, Asian and genealogy.

National Institutes of Health
NIH Office of Extramural Research
Minorities Training Programs

Internet: http://grants.nih.gov/training/minorities.htm

Offers links to organizations that offer grant money for minority-based research.

Smithsonian Institution
National Museum of the American Indian
Executive Offices

470 L'Enfant Plaza, SW

Suite 7102

Washington, DC 20560

Phone Research Center: (212) 514-3799

Internet: http://www.si.edu/nmai

The Smithsonian's National Museum of the American Indian is dedicated to the preservation, study, and exhibition of the life, languages, literature, history, and arts of Native Americans. Established by an Act of Congress in 1989, the museum works in collaboration with the Native peoples of the Western Hemisphere to protect and foster their cultures by reaffirming traditions and beliefs, encouraging contemporary artistic expression, and empowering the Indian voice.

White House Initiative on Tribal Colleges and Universities

Carrie L. Billy, Executive Director

Room 4050 MES

330 C. Street, SW, DC 20202-7594

Phone: (202) 260-5714

Fax: (202) 260-5702

E-mail: carrie_billy@ed.gov

Journals

American Indian Quarterly

American Indian Law Review

Ethnicity and Disease

2045 Manchester St. NW

Atlanta, GA 30324-4110

Phone: (404) 875-6263

Journal of Aging and Ethnicity

Springer Publishing Co.

536 Broadway

New York, NY 10012-3955

Journal of the Association of Academic Minority Physicians

Office of the Secretary
University of Maryland - School of Medicine
655 W. Baltimore St.
Baltimore, MD 21201
Phone: (410) 706-3100
Internet: www.ab.umd.edu

Journal for Minority Medical Students

Spectrum Unlimited
4203 Canal St.
New Orleans, LA 70019
Phone: (504) 488-5100
Internet: http://www.gnofn.org/~spectrum